I0751043

Faith

What? How? Whose?

By Karen M Gray

"*Faith: What, How, Whose?*" by Karen M Gray

Published by KMG Publications. Redland Bay, Queensland, Australia.
www.KMGPublications.com.au

Paperback Book: ISBN 978-0-9923543-6-7
Electronic Book: ISBN 978-0-9923543-7-4
HardCover Book: ISBN 978-0-9923543-8-1

Original cover concept: Karen M Gray.
Final printable production cover: "Billy Design @ khindir" operating from https://www.fiverr.com/khindir

Bible Quotes:

Dedication

~~~~~~~~~~~~~~~

This book is dedicated to the Bride of Christ. May she stand tall in the faith of God as we enter the last days of this current age.
~~~~~~~~~~~~~~~

Introduction

~~~~~~~~~~~~~~~

Faith, what exactly do we understand when we hear the word "faith"? No doubt we've all heard our share of sermons on the topic, and I'm sure we all have our own idea of what that word means. However, there's often some confusion because the word is used in various ways and contexts, and is often misused.

For me personally, I was always a little confused about the details. For example: "*Whose faith operates when a person stands in line for prayer?*", "*Is faith merely belief?*", and so on. I'd seen preachers blame people for their unbelief when healings do not happen, and also heard definitions of faith that never really satisfied my many questions surrounding the topic. I had had Hebrews 11:1 quoted to me, and various acronyms created from the letters of the word itself, but they still failed to answer all my questions. I even asked a pastor/teacher who ran a "school of the supernatural" but he couldn't answer either. It would appear that I was not the only one who was confused. However, if we are told by Jesus to "have faith", then surely, we need to be certain of exactly what it is that we should have, in order to fulfill this command!!

Then one day, while I studying the word in my own quiet time devotions, the Holy Spirit unexpectedly dropped a rhema word into my heart on the topic. From this starting point, together with more study into the topic from the scriptures, I pieced together a sermon on faith. However, it didn't stop there, as I realised this was a much bigger subject, drawing in topics of "hope", "love", "trust", "worship", and even "obedience" and "forgiveness". I would need
~~~~~~~~~~~~~~~

a series of sermons to cover the subject entirely. (You guessed it, I'm a teacher-preacher, and am pedantic about facts and details, and ensuring what I teach is completely in line with the word of God. Otherwise, I'm teaching opinions, which are basically worthless.)

Therefore, in this teaching, I'm hoping to clarify a few things and also share with you some revelations that God showed me along the way. In fact, I would say that most of this book is made from revelations that the Holy Spirit opened up to me in the Scriptures, and He even supplied me with some great examples and illustrations that would help you gain a clear grasp on the subject.

It is my hope that you are blessed in your faith as you read this! :)

Contents

~~~~~~~~~~~~~~~
~~~~~~~~~~~~~~~

Chapter 1:

A Clarification of Faith

~~~~~~~~~~~~~~~~

The Bible tells us plainly that the righteous/just shall live by faith:

> *"Behold the proud, his soul is not upright in him; but the just shall live by his faith."* – **Habakkuk 2:4 NKJV**

This is repeated by Paul in Romans and Galatians, and again by the author in Hebrews:

> *"For in it the righteousness of God is revealed from faith to faith; as it is written, 'The just shall live by faith.'"* – **Romans 1:17 NKJV**

> *"But that no one is justified by the law in the sight of God is evident, for "the just shall live by faith."* – **Galatians 3:13 NKJV**

> *"For yet a little while, and He who is coming will come and will not tarry. 'Now the just shall live by faith; but if anyone draws back, My soul has no pleasure in him.' But we are not of those who draw back to perdition, but of those who believe to the saving of the soul."* – **Hebrews 10:37-39 NKJV**

In each of these verses listed above and others, the authors use the quote in slightly different ways. That is:

* If we are proud, we will not be walking in faith but our own strength (Hab 2:4);

* If we live by faith, the righteousness of God will be
~~~~~~~~~~~~~~~~

seen through us (Rom 1:17);

* If we are righteous and live by faith, then we will have the law written on our hearts and automatically do what is right (Gal 3:13);

* We are expected to live by faith and not draw back in fear of those things happening around us, so that when the Lord Jesus returns, our souls are saved (Heb 10:37-39)

However, the issue here is not the way that the phrase is used by the New Testament writers, but that if we are to live by faith, what exactly does faith mean to us? How do we live by faith practically on a daily basis? & What exactly is faith?

Two Types of Faith

I want to take a quick look at how the Jewish believers interpret faith, because Jesus, being a Jew, would have been speaking from this perspective, even though He was also bringing in new elements to broaden the disciples understanding. But firstly, before I begin that, I'd quickly like to differentiate between THE faith and having faith IN something. Let me get that out of the way before I move on.

1) *THE Faith*

In Jude verse 3 Jude tells us to contend for the faith,

> "*Beloved, while I was very diligent to write to you concerning our common salvation, I found it necessary to write to you exhorting you to contend earnestly for the* ***faith*** *which was once for all delivered to the saints.*" – **Jude 1:3 NKJV**

In Jude's case, he was referring: **the teachings of Jesus, the doctrines and beliefs we hold as true**. Why, because Greek Gnosticism, (which relied upon "mystical knowledge" and believed the spiritual to be the only "good", and conversely, the material world was "evil"[1]) was proliferating all parts of the ancient world and had even crept into the church. It undermined the very fabric of the Word of God, was bringing complete error, and was ship wrecking people's salvation journey.

The other issue was that the Jewish Pharisaic believers were also upsetting the faith of many by their insistence that new believers come under the Law and be circumcised. This was because they did not have a full understanding of the New Covenant, but assumed the New Covenant was something to add to their existing faith. To them it was a continuation of the foundations Moses had already lain. Whilst Christianity was birthed out of the Jewish faith, we must remember that Christ Jesus came to fulfill the Law, that those who are now in Him (and thus, under the New Covenant) would have the Law also fulfilled for them through Him, and therefore, are no longer under the Law. The Law is now written on our hearts and is summed up by love. While we love both God and others, we are fulfilling the Law.

Jude rightly tells the flock to ensure that the Scripture and teachings of Jesus be strictly adhered to. He exhorted the brethren to hold tightly to the doctrines that they had been given, and not allow them to be distorted by well meaning

---

1 "Gnostics considered material existence flawed or evil, and held the principal element of salvation to be direct knowledge of the hidden divinity, attained via mystical or esoteric insight." – Wikipedia. Although I dislike using quotes from Wikipedia, it offered the most reasonable and concise definition. For more clarity on this topic, please see the descriptions from the following websites: https://www.learnreligions.com/what-is-gnosticism-700683, and https://iep.utm.edu/gnostic/.

"knowledgeable" men and teachers.

Moving on, we are also encouraged to "Stand Fast" in the faith.

> "*Watch,* ***stand fast in the faith****, be brave, be strong*" - **1 Corinthians 16:13 - NKJV**

In Philippians Paul talks about striving together for the faith:

> "*Only let your conduct be worthy of the gospel of Christ, so that whether I come and see you or am absent, I may hear of your affairs, that you stand fast in one spirit, with one mind* ***striving together for the faith*** *of the gospel*" – **Phil 1:27 NKJV**

And in Colossians, Paul encourages the brethren that now they've come this far, to continue in the faith, be steadfast, and not be moved from the gospel message that he preached to them.

> "*And you, who once were alienated and enemies in your mind by wicked works, yet now He has reconciled in the body of His flesh through death, to present you holy, and blameless, and above reproach in His sight—if indeed you* ***continue in the faith****, grounded and steadfast, and are not moved away from the hope of the gospel which you heard, which was preached to every creature under heaven, of which I, Paul, became a minister.*" – **Col 1:21-23 NKJV**

And later in the same letter he talks about being established in the faith,

> "*As you therefore have received Christ Jesus the Lord, so walk in Him, rooted and built up in Him and*

established in the faith*, as you have been taught, abounding in it with thanksgiving.*" **– Col 2:6,7 NKJV**

In other versions it says to be "grounded". (Same idea.)

Paul talks about the maturing of the body when it comes into the unity of the faith:

> "*...till we all come to the* ***unity of the faith*** *and of the knowledge of the Son of God, to a perfect man, to the measure of the stature of the fullness of Christ;*" – **Ephesians 4:13 NKJV**

That is, we all should hold the one doctrine and one faith, and not tossed about by other doctrines.

Paul also instructs us to examine whether we are in the faith lest we fall short.

> "*Examine yourselves as to whether you are* ***in the faith.*** *Test yourselves. Do you not know yourselves, that Jesus Christ is in you? - unless indeed you are disqualified.*" – **2 Corinthians 13:5 NKJV**

It is obvious from these Scripture verses that "*THE* Faith" is actually what we believe as a whole – **the things that Jesus taught us, and our doctrinal beliefs**. Extrapolating from there, we can see that the "faith*ful*" are those who *share* that same faith – the ones to whom Paul, the twelve apostles, and other church planters and leaders, are giving instructions and encouragements. These faithful are those who trust God enough to *follow* Jesus' instructions, and who *adhere* steadfastly to the Scriptures and gospel message of salvation.

OK! That's *THE* faith out of the way. I believe you are very clear on that. However, does this define "faith" as a whole?

Is HAVING faith the same as THE faith to which we adhere? The answer is, "NO!"

2) *To Have Faith*

Let's now look at what it means to have faith. You might be already quoting Hebrews 11:1 in your mind.

> "*Now faith is the substance of things hoped for, the evidence of things not seen.*" **– Hebrews 11:1 NKJV**

Whilst that's true of course, I want to first draw your attention to what Jesus teaches us about faith, and how He describes it. After all, Jesus commands us to have faith in God. (Mark 11:22-24). Therefore, we need to understand what exactly we need to have!

Was He telling us to accept a doctrine or reaffirmation of the things we believe? Not exactly, and this is where the confusion lies. Unfortunately, many of us are confused when it comes to an exact definition. We are like Donkey at the end of the first Shrek movie where he sings (professes), "I'm a believer!" Then, at the end of the song he sings repeatedly, "*I believe, I believe, I believe!!*"

We think that if we could just talk ourselves into believing enough, we can make things happen, or say to God, "*See, I believe enough that it's gonna happen.*" However, it's not about self-talk or convincing yourself that you believe. If you've merely convinced yourself that your built-up belief will cause things to happen, and they don't, you'll be left floundering, disappointed and confused. However, with absolute certainty I can tell you, that belief wasn't faith.

Nor is it about how much faith you have. How much faith do you really require to simply move a mountain? Faith, the size of a mustard seed. Let's take a closer look now at this passage about mustard seed faith. Just to place this in context, Jesus had cursed the fig tree the night before and on coming passed it again the next day, Peter checks it out. Then he remarks how the cursed tree has withered away. Let's pick up Jesus' response in verse 22:

> "*So, Jesus answered and said to them, "**Have faith** in God. For assuredly, I say to you, whoever says to this mountain, 'Be removed and be cast into the sea,' and does not doubt in his heart, but believes that those things he says will be done, he will have whatever he says. Therefore, I say to you, whatever things you ask when you pray, believe that you receive them, and you will have them.*" - **Mark 11:22-24 NKJV**

Some of you will no doubt say to me, "Look there! It says you must believe what you say before you can have what you say!" Whilst that is true, it's not the manifestation of the thing spoken that your belief should be centred upon, but rather, in the goodness of God to produce it. It's God's character that's the issue here. Rather than say to yourself, "*Wow! I don't think I could move a mountain! I don't think I have the faith to believe for that!*", look to God and say, "*If He said it, I believe in Him to do it, because what He says is absolutely true.*"

Not convinced? Then let's take a look at the parallel passage in Luke chapter 17 beginning at verse 5. The disciples asked Jesus to increase their faith, and Jesus responded by giving some teaching on the subject as well.

> "5 *And the apostles said to the Lord, "Increase our faith."*
> 6 *So the Lord said, "If you have faith as a mustard seed, you can say to this mulberry*[2] *tree, 'Be pulled up by the roots and be planted in the sea,' and it would obey you.*

"[7] And which of you, having a servant ploughing or tending sheep, will say to him when he has come in from the field, 'Come at once and sit down to eat'? [8] But will he not rather say to him, 'Prepare something for my supper, and gird yourself and serve me till I have eaten and drunk, and afterward you will eat and drink'? [9] Does he thank that servant because he did the things that were commanded him? I think not.

"[10] So likewise you, when you have done all those things which you are commanded, say, 'We are unprofitable servants. We have done what was our duty to do.'" – **Luke 17: 5-10 NKJV**

Jesus' response to the question of having enough faith (or increasing one's faith) was that even a mustard seed of faith can move mountains (or in this case a mulberry tree). That is, it's not the amount of faith that's the issue here but what your faith is based upon.

Jesus then continued on to talk about servants. Now, you might be inclined to think, '*Hang on a minute! He changed the topic without fully answering the question*', but He didn't. He is following up with an illustration. That is, in the same manner that you expect a servant to do what he is told without having to feed him up, build him up, reward him, or encourage him to do so, you don't need to bulk up your faith, or work it up somehow, in order for it to be done. That's not how it works.

---

2 The translation into "mulberry" tree is a poor translation that is not entirely accurate. Older Bible versions state it was a "sycamore" or "sycamine" tree, which is a far more faithful interpretation. The confusion occurs because the tree (ficus pseudo-sycomorus) is also known as a "mulberry-fig", and produces leaves similar to a mulberry tree, but has small round reddish in appearance, fruit that grows in clusters, and that some people claim look similar to figs. They are not mulberries, nor are they in any way related. The tree has very deep roots and holds fast to the ground. Thus, the point here is that uprooting such a tree is extremely difficult but those with faith can move it with ease.

(Now some people might wish to remind me here that Pastors often try and build up people's faith, especially prior to a healing/miracle service. However, the testimonies are not given to convince you that if you believe enough, then you'll receive, but that you will be encouraged by what God has done for others and how He, because of His generosity and love toward you, wants to do these things for you too. Testimonies build your faith in God.)

Going back to Jesus's illustration regarding a servant: In a similar fashion to the servant carrying out a command his master gives him, we likewise, when God tells us to do something, whether it's to command a mountain to be removed, or to pray for the sick, we are expected to be obedient.

That might sound harsh BUT the good news is that we can be assured that the outcome will be in God's favour because *He* wants it done, and because His hand is on it to *make* it happen. Therefore, He will supply all that's required for us to complete the task. We just do it and it works. It has nothing to do with us. We are just the hands and feet that He uses. Sure, we show our badges of authority in Christ to the enemy (declaring "*In Jesus Name*"), but in the end, we are just like the unprofitable servant, privileged enough to work with Him, but still just the servants after all. Yes, He delights to work with us, but in the end it's God who gets the glory.

The Chain of Command

It's important to understand that there's a pecking order in the spirit realm. God and His word have the last say and are the ultimate authority. You have also been given authority and are seated with Christ in heavenly places. This authority is a result of the New Covenant. It's no longer I who lives but Christ who lives in me (Gal 2:20), and just as He is, so I am in this world, (1John 4:17)! Now even the demons are subject to us, and also the natural world must obey us, but still, we are also under His authority. There's a command structure in place. Once we understand this, it can make things much simpler.

Consider the Roman centurion with the sick servant (Matthew 8:5-13; Luke 7:2-10). He sent message to Jesus, as Jesus was walking towards his house, that there was no need for Him to actually visit to the house. He understood the command structure. He can tell his servants to go and they go. He himself was also under authority. If someone more senior than he, told him to do something, he knew he couldn't argue the point, he had to go and do it.

The centurion, likewise knew that Jesus had ultimate authority and power to back it up. If Jesus told the illness to go, it was out of there quick smart – no "if's", "but's" or "maybe's". Jesus then commended this man for his faith. He understood how it all worked.

Consider also another non-Jew, whom Jesus actually commended for her faith. She was the Canaanite woman, who kept pestering Jesus to cast out the demon that was afflicting her daughter. This is an interesting case so I'd like to look at in a little depth.

> *"Then Jesus went out from there and departed to the region of Tyre and Sidon. And behold, a woman of Canaan came from that region and cried out to Him, saying, "Have mercy on me, O Lord, Son of David! My daughter is severely demon-possessed."*
>
> *But He answered her not a word. And His disciples*

came and urged Him, saying, "Send her away, for she cries out after us." But He answered and said, "I was not sent except to the lost sheep of the house of Israel."

Then she came and worshiped Him, saying, "Lord, help me!" But He answered and said, "It is not good to take the children's bread and throw it to the little dogs." And she said, "Yes, Lord, yet even the little dogs eat the crumbs which fall from their masters' table." Then Jesus answered and said to her, "O woman, great is your faith! Let it be to you as you desire." And her daughter was healed from that very hour."" – **Matthew 15:21-28 NKJV**

The interesting thing here is that Jesus was not being racist for not wanting to heal her daughter. He had healed others who were not Jewish, (take the previous example of Jesus healing the Roman Centurion's servant). So, why did He ignore her for so long and then treat her the way He did? Some will answer that He was testing her faith, but was that all that was going on? I would say, "*No!*" Let's take a deeper examination of what's happening here!

Note, that Jesus talks about the "*children's bread*". Who are the children to which He refers? I do not believe they are simply the children of Israel, and everyone else from other nations are considered "dogs". Besides the fact that that remark would be therefore, totally racist, it is definitely ***not*** in keeping with Jesus' message, nor His mission to promote the gospel to all men. Exclusivism was definitely not something He espoused - quite the opposite, in fact! Thus, the true children here, are those who have given over their lives into His hands, and follow Him with their whole heart. They are true believers – sons and daughters of God.

This woman was from a pagan nation. She had obviously

heard about Jesus and His miracle working power. (Remember that multitudes followed Him. One example was when He fed the five thousand – that was just the head count of the men present. You could easily double that figure when you factor in the women and children present there too. This massive following was not unusual. Multitudes followed Him everywhere. He was famous, and attracted the attention even of the Romans, and this was giving the religious leaders reason to be nervous.) If this foreigner had not heard about all Jesus had done, she would hardly have approached Him. However, although she believed He could help her daughter, there is nothing recorded to indicate that she was willing to turn from her pagan beliefs in order to follow Jesus. She merely wanted a freebie.

You may be thinking, '*But look there in verse 25, it says she worshipped Jesus.*' The word that has been translated as "*worshipped*", is the Greek word, "*proskuneo*" (Strong's 4352), and is used to indicate an act of homage or reverence. That is, the woman bowed down before Jesus, because she is pleading with Him to heal her daughter! It doesn't mean she had any desire to follow Him or glorify Him, but that she understood He was the only man who could help her. She was desperate.

As such, Jesus explained that this miracle working power wasn't for those who were not, or would not, become children of God, nor was it fair to the children to have their bread (what is rightfully theirs) thrown to the dogs. Nevertheless, she was unswayed in her determination. He was the only person who could help. She had heard the stories and wouldn't take "No!" for an answer. Thus, she answered that even the dogs eat the crumbs from the children's table. Her faith in Jesus to heal her daughter was doggedly (excuse the pun) determined. She wouldn't leave until He agreed to do this, and as a result, Jesus agreed to her request and healed her daughter.

It was not that the Canaanite woman was a follower of Christ that Jesus granted this request, but that she believed that Jesus was both able and would do it for her. In her mind He was the spiritual boss. He was the heavenly man in charge, and as such what He said goes! This then, is the kind of faith Jesus is looking for in us: determined to keep looking at the One who is able to do far above all we ask and think, and also determined not to let go until we have the miracle we seek.

Returning to our passage in Luke, this is also what Jesus is trying to point out to the disciples. It's not the amount of faith they need. They had to change the way they looked at God, and His spiritual chain of command. Faith is about His authority in the spirit realm, knowing the will of God, and knowing our place under Him. We are just the jumper leads from the source – Christ in us – to whomever requires a touch from God. If God says, lay hands on the sick and they will recover, then He's the boss. What He says happens with no arguments, unless our faith blocks the way and causes a faulty connection.

Do we have faith that God is who He says He is, or are we putting our faith in "how well", or "how much" we believe? Let's take a look at Mark 4:35-41

> "*On the same day, when evening had come, He said to them, "Let us cross over to the other side." Now when they had left the multitude, they took Him along in the boat as He was. And other little boats were also with Him.*
>
> *And a great windstorm arose, and the waves beat into*

the boat, so that it was already filling. But He was in the stern, asleep on a pillow. And they awoke Him and said to Him, "Teacher, do You not care that we are perishing?"

Then He arose and rebuked the wind, and said to the sea, "Peace, be still!" And the wind ceased and there was a great calm. But He said to them, "Why are you so fearful? How is it that you have no faith?" And they feared exceedingly, and said to one another, "Who can this be, that even the wind and the sea obey Him!" - **Mark 4:35-41 NKJV**

When Jesus took His disciples out in the boat to cross over to the other side, it had been a tiring day. The multitudes had been following them around, and as usual He had taught them, healed them and cast out demons. Jesus was tired enough to crash on a cushion and fall asleep in the back of the boat.

Then out of nowhere, a huge storm blew up as they were out at sea, causing the waves to crash over the boat and the water to start filling it. Even though the disciples were seasoned fishermen, (no doubt they'd been out fishing in all kinds of weather), the storm became so bad that they became fearful. When they finally remembered that their Master was asleep in the back of the boat, the first thing they said to Him was, "*Don't You care that we are perishing?*" It was like an accusation. Things weren't working out for them so it must be God's fault! Isn't He supposed to be looking after them? (How many of us have we thought the same?)

Jesus then stood up and rebuked the storm, and turned and rebuked them for their *lack* of faith. *They* were trying to deal with the situation. As fishermen, they must have dealt with storms before, but they hadn't expected, nor anticipated, a storm to well up suddenly, and swamp the boat with such ferocity.

Why was this happening to them? WRONG question! What did they have faith in? Did Jesus ever say there would be a life without suffering or tribulation? No! BUT they should have had faith in Him. He should have been their first "go-to". "*Master what should we do?*" should have been their reaction, rather than trying to fix the problem themselves first, and then when they couldn't fix the problem in their own strength, blaming Him for not caring.

God is able to do far more than we can imagine.

> "*Him who is able to do exceedingly abundantly above all that we ask or think, according to the power that works in us*" - **Ephesians 3:20 NKJV**

There is nothing God cannot do.

> "*For with God nothing [is or ever] shall be impossible.*" – **Luke 1:37 AMP**

In Mark 14:36, Jesus' prayer at Gethsemane began like this,

> "*Abba, Father, all things are possible for You.*"

Jesus knew His Father had absolute power and authority. Further, all things are possible to those who believe. Believe not in your abilities, but in His.

> "*Jesus said to him, "If you can believe, all things are possible to him who believes.*" – **Mark 9:23 NKJV**

It comes down to "where?", "in what?", and "in who?" we place our faith. The problem is that we have this big question looming larger than life that stops us believing. That is: "*Yeah, I get it, but will He do it for* ***me****? After all, look at what a miserable Christian I am.*"

Here in lies the biggest hurdle to our faith. Real faith depends on how well we recognise and understand the absolute goodness and love of the Father towards us, AND our *identity* in Christ. (More on this aspect of faith in later chapters.)

At this point, if you didn't already, you should understand the spiritual command structure and that God has ultimate power and authority. However, you might be asking, "How does this play out practically if I'm personally praying for something? What does it look like to have faith then?" Let's explore just that.

Personal Requests

There are two possible alternatives when we make a request to God, and these will, in part at least, determine our answer:

a) It's promised in His Word,

b) It's not in the Word.

a) When It's Promised in The Bible

If it's a promise in the Bible, then you can be sure that you have it when you ask for it in faith, because God's word is absolutely true. He is faithful to His word, and therefore, it's yours because He said it is. You want healing, it's already promised, and He is faithful. The healing is yours. You can expect it when you ask for it. You can even picture it in your mind. It may not be instant but it's on the way. In fact, acting like you already have it, shows God that you trust Him and His Word as dependable and true, and He delights in that. As Christians we are expected to have faith in Him and His word.

Repeatedly, the Bible tells us to trust God, or to have faith in God. It also instructs us to believe in Him. Plus, the Bible also states that there are benefits to having faith in and trusting in Him, and that He delights in those that do. Suffice to say, the list of these Bible verses is quite long, so please bear with me. I've included many of them to bring this point home.

> "*So, they rose early in the morning and went out into the Wilderness of Tekoa; and as they went out, Jehoshaphat stood and said, "Hear me, O Judah and you inhabitants of Jerusalem:* ***Believe in the LORD your God****, and you shall be established; believe His prophets, and you shall prosper.*" - **2 Chronicles 20:20 NKJV**

> "*Jesus answered and said to them, "This is the work of God, that you* ***believe in Him*** *whom He sent.*"" - **John 6:29 NKJV**

> "*Jesus heard that they had cast him out; and when He had found him, He said to him, 'Do you* ***believe in the Son of God****?' He answered and said, 'Who is He, Lord, that I may* ***believe in Him****?*'" - **John 9:35-36 NKJV**

> "*While you have the light, believe in the light, that you may become sons of light." These things Jesus spoke, and departed, and was hidden from them. But although He had done so many signs before them, they did not* ***believe in Him***" - **John 12:36-37 NKJV**

> "***Trust in the LORD****, and do good; Dwell in the land,*

and feed on His faithfulness." **- Psalm 37:3 NKJV**

"***Trust in Him*** *at all times, you people; Pour out your heart before Him; God is a refuge for us. Selah"* - **Psalm 62:8 NKJV**

"But it is good for me to draw near to God; I have put my ***trust in the Lord GOD****, That I may declare all Your works."* **- Psalm 73:28 NKJV**

"O Israel, ***trust in the LORD;*** *He is their help and their shield. O house of Aaron,* ***trust in the LORD;*** *He is their help and their shield. You who fear the LORD,* ***trust in the LORD;*** *He is their help and their shield."* **- Psalm 115:9-11 NKJV**

"***Trust in the LORD*** *with all your heart, And lean not on your own understanding;"* **- Prov 3:5 NKJV**

"***Trust in the LORD*** *forever, for in YAH, the LORD, is everlasting strength."* **- Isaiah 26:4 NKJV**

"But you denied the Holy One and the Just, and asked for a murderer to be granted to you, and killed the Prince of Life, whom God raised from the dead, of which we are witnesses. And His name, through ***faith in His name****, has made this man strong, whom you see and know. Yes, the* ***faith which comes through Him*** *has given him this perfect soundness in the presence of you all."* **- Acts 3:14-16 NKJV**

"As for God, His way is perfect; The word of the LORD is proven; He is a shield to all who ***trust in Him****."* **- Psalm 18:30 NKJV**

"Some trust in chariots and some in horses, but we ***trust in the name of the LORD our God****."* - Psalm

20:7 NIV

"*O my God, **I trust in You**; Let me not be ashamed; Let not my enemies triumph over me.*" - **Psalm 25:2 NKJV**

"*Keep my soul, and deliver me; Let me not be ashamed, for I put my **trust in You**.*" - **Psalm 25:20 NKJV**

"*I have hated those who regard useless idols; But I **trust in the LORD**.*" - **Psalm 31:6 NKJV**

"*But as for me, **I trust in You, O LORD**; I say, "You are my God.*"" - **Psalm 31:14 NKJV**

"*Oh, how great is Your goodness, Which You have laid up for those who fear You, Which You have prepared for those who **trust in You** In the presence of the sons of men!*" - **Psalm 31:19 NKJV**

"*The LORD redeems the soul of His servants, and none of those who **trust in Him** shall be condemned.*" - **Psalm 34:22 NKJV**

"*And the LORD shall help them and deliver them; He shall deliver them from the wicked, and save them, because they **trust in Him**.*" - **Psalm 37:40 NKJV**

"*He has put a new song in my mouth— Praise to our God; Many will see it and fear, and will **trust in the LORD**.*" - **Psalm 40:3 NKJV**

"*But You, O God, shall bring them down to the pit of destruction; Bloodthirsty and deceitful men shall not live out half their days; But I will **trust in You**.*" - **Psalm 55:23 NKJV**

"*Whenever I am afraid, I will **trust in You**.*" - **Psalm**

56:3 NKJV

"*The righteous shall be glad in the LORD, and **trust in Him**. And all the upright in heart shall glory.*" - **Psalm 64:10 NKJV**

"*It is better to **trust in the LORD** Than to put confidence in man. It is better to trust in the LORD Than to put confidence in princes.*" - **Psalm 118:8,9 NKJV**

"*Those who **trust in the LORD** are like Mount Zion, which cannot be moved, but abides forever.*" - **Psalm 125:1 NKJV**

"*Every word of God is pure; He is a shield to those who put their **trust in Him**.*" - **Proverbs 30:5 NKJV**

"*The word of the LORD is proven; He is a shield to all who **trust in Him**.*" - **2 Samual 22:31 NKJV**

"*And they were helped against them, and the Hagrites were delivered into their hand, and all who were with them, for they cried out to God in the battle. He heeded their prayer, because they put their **trust in Him**.*" - **1 Chronicles 5:20**

"*Kiss the Son, lest He be angry, and you perish in the way, when His wrath is kindled but a little. Blessed are all those who put their **trust in Him**.*" - **Psalm 2:12 NKJV**

"*Offer the sacrifices of righteousness, and put your **trust in the LORD**.*" - **Psalm 4:5 NKJV**

"*But let all those rejoice who put their **trust in You**; Let them ever shout for joy, because You defend them; Let those also who love Your name. Be joyful in You.*" -

Psalm 5:11 NKJV

"*And those who know Your name will put their* ***trust in You****; For You, LORD, have not forsaken those who seek You.*" - **Psalm 9:10 NKJV**

"*Show Your marvellous lovingkindness by Your right hand, O You who save those who* ***trust in You*** *From those who rise up against them.*" - **Psalm 17:7 NKJV**

"*For you are all sons of God through* ***faith in Christ Jesus****.*" - **Galatians 3:26**

"*But now the righteousness of God apart from the law is revealed, being witnessed by the Law and the Prophets, even the righteousness of God, through* ***faith in Jesus Christ****, to all and on all who believe.*" – **Romans 3:21-22 NKJV**

"*We who are Jews by nature, and not sinners of the Gentiles knowing that a man is not justified by the works of the law but by* ***faith in Jesus Christ****, even we have believed in Christ Jesus, that we might be justified by* ***faith in Christ*** *and not by the works of the law; for by the works of the law no flesh shall be justified. But if, while we seek to be justified by Christ, we ourselves also are found sinners, is Christ therefore a minister of sin? Certainly not! For if I build again those things which I destroyed, I make myself a transgressor. For I through the law died to the law that I might live to God. "I have been crucified with Christ; it is no longer I who live, but Christ lives in me; and the life which I now live in the flesh I live by* ***faith in the Son of God****, who loved me and gave Himself for me.*" – **Galatians 2:15-20 NKJV**

"But the Scripture has confined all under sin, that the promise by ***faith in Jesus Christ*** *might be given to those who believe."* - **Galatians 3:22 NKJV**

"Therefore, I also, after I heard of your ***faith in the Lord Jesus*** *and your love for all the saints"* - **Ephesians 1:15 NKJV**

"This was according to the eternal purpose that he has realized in Christ Jesus our Lord, in whom we have boldness and access with confidence through our ***faith in Him.****"* - **Ephesians 3:11-12 ESV**

"We give thanks to the God and Father of our Lord Jesus Christ, praying always for you, since we heard of your faith in Christ Jesus and of your love for all the saints" – **Colossians 1:3-4 NKJV**

"In Him you were also circumcised with the circumcision made without hands, by putting off the body of the sins of the flesh, by the circumcision of Christ, buried with Him in baptism, in which you also were raised with Him through ***faith in the working of God****, who raised Him from the dead."* – **Colossians 2:11-12 NKJV**

"I do not pray for these alone, but also for those who will ***believe in Me*** *through their word"* - **John 17:20 NKJV**

"It shall be imputed to us who ***believe in Him*** *who raised up Jesus our Lord from the dead"*- **Romans 4:24 NKJV**

"For to you it has been granted on behalf of Christ, not only to ***believe in Him****, but also to suffer for His sake"* – **Philippians 1:29 NKJV**

Why does the Bible repeatedly record these verses telling us to have faith in Him, to believe in Him and to trust in Him? Surely, because it emphasizes this repeatedly, we need to take notice! Our faith must be solidly in God, Himself, and not in how much faith we have in faith, nor in how much we believe the answer will magically appear because we've prayed, nor because we believe we do or don't deserve to have our requests answered.

For example: Imagine you are a young teenager and your father tells you he'll buy you a new car up to a certain value once you pass your driving license test. Do you think,

> '*Well, I don't know about that. Perhaps I'm not good enough. Perhaps I haven't spent enough time with him. Or perhaps I'm the worst child he has and he merely tolerates me. Why would he give me a car?*"

NO!!! If your dad made you a promise, you'd be online checking out all the cars available within the financial budget he had specified. You'd read up all the reviews and how much it would cost you to maintain. And when you found one that suited all your requirements, you'd probably go and check out something similar (if not the car) at the local car yard. Then once you have it settled in your mind, you'd be imagining about what it was going to be like once you had your car, how it will change things for you, and even how your friends will drool over it once you drive it to school or to some social gathering.

More so, we can trust our Heavenly Father to fulfil His promises to us. He won't give us a scorpion when we ask for an egg. (Luke 11:12) The egg speaks of newness, promise and expectancy, and the scorpion – the sting of disappointment. He knows how to give good gifts to His people and He's far above any earthly father.

Not only do we trust Him because it's in His Word, but we can trust Him because we know Him personally. We know what He is like and how dependable He is. People don't just put their trust in any old thing. Their trust is *built upon* a foundation of experience and knowing a person's character. The more we know Him, the more we love and trust Him. This is where reading the word to renew your mind to understand how He thinks, and being intimate & worshipping Him personally, are so very important, even essential, to your faith.

As briefly mentioned, we don't have "faith in faith", but have faith in the character and goodness *of God*. He said it, it's a done deal! Smith Wigglesworth said, "*He said it, I believe it, that settles it!*" It's all about Him - His truthfulness, His goodness and His love. It's not about us! Therefore, if you believe you have those things you requested *because of who God is*, and that what He has said will come to pass, then you will have them. It's all about His character and His truthfulness.

b) When It's Not in The Bible

What if the things for which we are asking God, are not promised in the Bible? Obviously, you inquire of God whether it is His will or not. Now if you have renewed your mind in the word, you will likely already have an inkling of what way the answer will fall. Most likely God will grant your request when you have faith, because He is a good and generous Father, but He also wants what's best for us. Therefore, we ask.

Once we know we have the things for which we petitioned God – i.e., we know that we know, that God has answered, "Yes!" to our request – then we become grateful and act like we have it. We can call forth those things that are not as though they already were. We start to act like we have it in the same way that the son with the promise of a new car is preparing to receive it on the day! We do this because it's a done deal. We can begin to act like it's on the way.

For example: When I order something online, I have faith that it will be delivered, because that's part of their promise/service once the item is paid for. (Well, there are obvious flaws in this analogy because people sometimes make mistakes, but on the whole, I know that it will be delivered.) Now, if God has said, "Yes!" to our request and we have made certain of this, what we've requested is in the spirit mail. We can act as though it's being delivered. We have those things that we requested and it's just a matter of time before it comes. Why? Because we know the Faithful One with whom we've made the request, and know His answer and that His word is true and final. We can start acting as if it's in our hand.

What if God says, "*No!*" to your request? It's possible that what you are asking for is not in your best interests to have. We can't always see the bigger picture. We need to humble and submit to His will not ours –just like Jesus at Gethsemane.

> "*And He said, 'Abba, Father, all things are possible for You. Take this cup away from Me; nevertheless, not what I will, but what You will.'*" – **Matthew 14:26 NKJV**
>
> "*And He was withdrawn from them about a stone's throw, and He knelt down and prayed, saying, 'Father, if it is Your will, take this cup away from Me; nevertheless, not My will, but Yours, be done.'*" – **Luke 22:41-42 NKJV**

God's will was *not* to take the cup of suffering from Him.

Jesus did not want to suffer under the brutality and cruelty of the Romans, but nonetheless, He humbly submitted to God's will, despite what He knew He would have to endure.

What if you can't hear the answer – is God saying "Yes!" or "No!"? Rather than answer that here, I will discuss in some length in the next chapter, ways that enable you to hear more accurately from God.

Not What You Say, But How You Say it

Just a note here: If we ask whilst whingeing and grumbling, or even blaming God, or even demanding He fulfil His promises, will He answer? Put yourself in that position. If someone wanted something from you and their attitude was to constantly whine and complain, and even blame you that things are in a particular state, or grumble that you haven't given them what they wanted when they wanted it, would you feel much like granting their petition? I don't know how you would answer, but I personally would feel like running away in the opposite direction. (Of course, everyone's tolerance and grace levels are different. Thankfully God's love is enormous and His grace is abundant.) However, He has already given us all we need for life and Godliness, and that life in abundance:

> "*His divine power has given to us all things that pertain to life and godliness, through the knowledge of Him who called us by glory and virtue, by which have been given to us exceedingly great and precious promises, that through these you may be partakers of the divine nature, having escaped the corruption that is in the world through lust.*" - **2 Peter 1:3-4 NKJV**

> "*I have come that they may have life, and that they may have it more abundantly.*" - **John 10:10b NKJV**

With such great abundance and promises, there is no need to complain. In fact, what right do we have to complain? We are blessed far beyond those who are unsaved. Perhaps not in the material realm, but definitely with all the spiritual blessings,

> "*Blessed be the God and Father of our Lord Jesus Christ, who has blessed us with every spiritual blessing in the heavenly places in Christ*" – **Ephesians 1:3 NKJV**

Plus, even though we may consider ourselves as having very little, He has promised to give us all we need.

> "*Then He said to His disciples, "Therefore I say to you, do not worry about your life, what you will eat; nor about the body, what you will put on. Life is more than food, and the body is more than clothing.*
>
> *"Consider the ravens, for they neither sow nor reap, which have neither storehouse nor barn; and God feeds them. Of how much more value are you than the birds? And which of you by worrying can add one cubit to his stature? If you then are not able to do the least, why are you anxious for the rest?*
>
> *"Consider the lilies, how they grow: they neither toil nor spin; and yet I say to you, even Solomon in all his glory was not arrayed like one of these. If then God so clothes the grass, which today is in the field and tomorrow is thrown into the oven, how much more will He clothe you, O you of little faith?*
>
> *"And do not seek what you should eat or what you should drink, nor have an anxious mind. For all these things the nations of the world seek after, and your Father knows that you need these things. But seek the*

> *kingdom of God, and all these things shall be added to you.*
>
> *"Do not fear, little flock, for it is your Father's good pleasure to give you the kingdom. Sell what you have and give alms; provide yourselves money bags which do not grow old, a treasure in the heavens that does not fail, where no thief approaches nor moth destroys. For where your treasure is, there your heart will be also."* – **Luke 12:22-34 NKJV**

Peter also tells us that we have been given everything we need.

> *"His divine power has given to us all things that pertain to life and godliness, through the knowledge of Him who called us by glory and virtue."* – 2 Peter 1:3 NKJV

There is no room to complain, only to rejoice and be thankful as we seek His Kingdom. We can enter His gates with thanksgiving even when we don't get our own way, because He has everything for us that our life requires when it is required.

> *"Enter into His gates with thanksgiving, and into His courts with praise. Be thankful to Him, and bless His name."* - **Psalm 100:4 NKJV**

Obviously, the correct way to come before our King and Lord is to enter His courts with thanksgiving and praise, and in humility. Besides which, He deserves our respect!! A bad attitude before God means there's something not right with your relationship with Him.

He is absolutely perfect in every way, and His love far exceeds anything known to mankind. So, who is the one at fault in this complaining situation? Sometimes we need to take a heart check before we ask God anything. Do we ask as someone who loves God above all else, even ourselves, OR do we love ourselves before anyone else - even God? When the former is the answer, your attitude for petitioning God will be correct.

The Faith Definition

As promised in the initial pages of this book, I'd now like to take a broader look at faith. We need a clearer definition, and that can in part be found in Hebrews 11.

> "*Now faith is the substance of things hoped for, the evidence of things not seen.*" - **Hebrews 11:1 NKJV**

We may have some ideas as to what is meant by that verse, but Jesus was a Jew and His disciples and audience at the time were also Jews. How did they understand faith, and does it align with the verse in Hebrews listed above?

The Jewish Perspective

Note: This definition was given to me by a Messianic Jew, but I believe they have pieced it together from an article at https://www.myjewishlearning.com/article/emunah-biblical-faith

> **Jewish Definition**: Faithfulness, faith - "Emunah". (Pronounced: eh-moo-NAH)
>
> Meaning: A relationship.
>
> Origin: Hebrew and is all about how we walk.
>
> Discussion: "Emet" on the other hand means

"Truth" - as in God is Truth. Unfortunately, this word is often confused by non-Jews as "*Emunah*".

In Genesis 15:6, what is the nature of Abraham's faith in God, that was counted as "righteousness"? In this verse "*Tzedah*", means "righteousness" or "justice" and is one of the attributes of the LORD God of Israel. God is called the "*LORD our Righteousness*", or the "*Righteous Judge*". There's also the Righteous God, and so on.

It is quite clear that Abraham's righteous belief was not as simply accepting God's statements as true, but by doing (Abram went into his wife Sarah, and as he went, he walked into the future) Abram did what Almighty had said.

The "*Emunah*", walking out, spoken of here is more than belief that certain statements about God are true; it is belief in God, Himself, trust and reliance upon God, all of which call forth behaviour consistent with that stance of trust and reliance.

The meaning of "*emunah*" is neither new nor controversial; it is just not often applied. We, the body of Messiah, talk a lot about praying and proclaiming the Scriptures, but not physically walking that out. Examining the verses in context is enough to convince any reader that the basic root meaning of "*emunah*" is action to walk forward towards the face, the Panim of Elohim. Being a doer and not a hearer only. Forsaking what is behind and moving towards the face-to-face relationship we were born for."

The word "faith" occurs 49 times in the Old Testament, but the meaning differs slightly depending on the context.

Thus, I am adding some further definitions retrieved from Biblehub.com:

Lexical Summary:

emunah: Faithfulness, fidelity, steadfastness, trust, faith

Original Word: הָנוּמֱא

Part of Speech: Noun Feminine

Transliteration: emuwnah

Pronunciation: eh-moo-nah

Phonetic Spelling: (em-oo-naw')

KJV: faith(-ful, -ly, -ness, (man)), set office, stability, steady, truly, truth, verily

NASB: faithfulness, faithfully, truth, faithful, trust, faith, honestly

Word Origin: [feminine of H529 (ןוּמֵא - faithful)]

1. literally firmness
2. figuratively security
3. morally fidelity

Strong's Exhaustive Concordance:

faithful set office, stability, steady, truly, truth, verily

NAS Exhaustive Concordance:

Word Origin from aman

Definition: firmness, steadfastness, fidelity

We tend to get fixated on the "*I believe, I believe, I believe!!!*" part, instead of trusting in His authority and His desire to give you what you requested. True faith is stable, steadfast and secure, and does not waver to and fro. In addition, we often forget to walk it out – to put legs on our faith. It's important act like you have what's coming to you. (e.g. When you receive a prayer of healing, do something you couldn't do before - act like you are healed. If your back had been too sore to move before it was prayed over, try moving it, and so on.) Instead, we get hung up on incorrect notions like,

> "*Oh, I haven't prayed enough this week.*" Or
>
> "*I had that unkind thought about that person yesterday, so God is probably miffed at me.*" Or
>
> "*Why would God give me – a measly worm – anything?*"

These are just lies of the enemy. The enemy wants you to lose faith in God, and ultimately, your relationship with Him. (Note: In the end, you'll get what you believe for – positive or negative.) If you believe the lies of the enemy, your faith will be eroded away. It doesn't happen in an instant but through a series of little disappointments. Before you know it, you will no longer be a follower of Christ Jesus our Lord and Saviour. Countless people have walked away from God and Christianity because of this.

Faith, Belief, Trust & Knowledge

I'd like to now differentiate between faith, belief, and trust as understood in the Bible. While they are similar, they do have slight differences. You will have first noticed that the long list of Scripture verses I quoted previously contain all three words. So how does that change things?

I have already defined "faith" as knowing God well enough to know that what He says is 100% true because He is not a man that He should lie. It is not a head knowledge (though it may start there and through revelation translate into our spirit man) but a heart knowledge. You know that you know, that you know, what God commands is done. You are fully convinced even though you may not be able to see the manifestation yet. You are so convinced that you walk it out as if it was visible/manifest already.

Belief is giving mental ascent to something. You agree that it is true. You may, or may not have even seen evidence to support this belief, but you agree in your mind that it is true and plausible. As far as you're concerned, it is so.

Belief could be seen as the beginning of faith. We believe something to be true, but as time goes by, the supporting experiences accumulate, and our intimacy with God continues to build. It is then that our belief moves from just a head knowledge, to knowing the character of God, which then translates into a heart knowledge. At this point there is no possibility in your mind and heart that He is incorrect, or has not spoken anything but truth. Your heart is tied to His, and you know beyond any shadow of a doubt, that He cares for you. Why, because He has spoken it so often (and does not lie) and He has shown you His love time and time again to backup/prove His words.

Just how much we know someone can easily be seen in how we **trust** them. The more we know them and have life experiences with them, the more trust is nurtured and grown. In the case of trusting God, trust is built on knowing

God, but it's also knowing how *valuable* we are in His eyes. How can we say we love God and then say we don't trust *His love* for us?

To illustrate this, think of a newly married couple. Does the bride trust her husband to treat her well? Yes! Is the bride important in his eyes? Yes! Does the bride ever expect that her groom will act like an angry task master towards her? No! Does she think her groom will not follow through with his promises? No! Why? Because he loves her and has become one with her. Further, we are the Bride of Christ and He is one with us. As previously quoted:

> "*I have been crucified with Christ;* ***it is no longer I who live, but Christ lives in me****; and the life which I now live in the flesh I live by faith in the Son of God, who loved me and gave Himself for me.*" - **Galatians 2:20 NKJV**

We trust in God because we know Him well. He is always faithful to us. He is dependable, reliable, gives us strength when we are week, lifts us up and dusts us off when we fall, encourages us to try again when we fail, is the author and finisher of our lives, and willing to grant us any requests that align with His plans and purposes to that end. He is our best friend that we can call in times of need, and He hears.

In fact, in Luke 11, Jesus tells us that asking God for something is like going to a friend at night to obtain some bread to feed a late visitor to your home. Now a normal friend might object because of the lateness of the hour, and that he's in bed and so is the family, but on your insistence and persistence, he'll get up and give you what you've asked for because he is your friend. Jesus is our friend as well. In fact, closer than a friend. Therefore, He tells us to keep knocking until the door is open and we've received what we've asked for.

It's like asking your earthly father for something, (though remember that our heavenly Father is far superior to our earthly ones). Our earthly parents may know how to give good things to their children even if they are evil, but our heavenly Father is all good, and knows how to give good gifts (Matthew 7:11) and even the Holy Spirit (Luke 11:13) to those who ask Him. We just need to keep on knocking, be persistent and realise what is taking place in the spirit realm, trusting in God's good character, not our bad one. We CAN trust Him above everything else – just like a child trusts his father to give him what he needs and to take care of him. We can have faith like a child.

How does trust differ from faith? Trust is knowing that God will never hurt you. Everything will turn out for good to those who love and serve Him.

> "*And we know that all things work together for good to those who love God, to those who are the called according to His purpose.*" - **Romans 8:28 NKJV**

Conversely, faith is knowing that what He said is absolute truth, and therefore, what we have asked for, whether material or spiritual, (knowing that we asked within His will and not amiss), will indeed manifest as we wait on Him. Note: Both faith and trust rely on how well we know our God, and how much we love our Bridegroom.

How can We Ask in Complete Trust?

When Paul wrote in a letter to Timothy, he reminds Timothy to pray without doubting in God or His goodness.

> *"I desire therefore that the men pray everywhere, lifting up holy hands, without wrath and doubting"* – **1 Timothy 2:8 NKJV**

Note: that lifting up holy hands also suggests that we are praying with adoration, praise and worship, because we know that God is good all the time, no matter how things might appear. Praise and worship help to break the yolk. When we delight ourselves in God, He gives us the desires of our heart.

> *"Delight yourself also in the LORD, and He shall give you the desires of your heart."* – **Psalm 37:4 NKJV**

Besides which, praise and worship in the midst of turmoil demonstrates to God our trust and faith in Him, and it pleases Him greatly. It can also give us a peace knowing that everything is bound to work out. So, there's no down side, only plusses.

Remember what happened to Paul and Silas as they sang praises to God whilst being incarcerated and held in stocks. We do not know whether they had prayed for a quick release, but we do know they trusted God would make all things turn out for good, because that's what God does, i.e. good for those who love Him. We read the story in Acts 16: 16-40, but the main verses are these:

> *"Then the multitude rose up together against them; and the magistrates tore off their clothes and commanded them to be beaten with rods. And when they had laid many stripes on them, they threw them into prison, commanding the jailer to keep them securely. Having received such a charge, he put them into the inner prison and fastened their feet in the stocks. But at midnight Paul and Silas were praying and singing hymns*

to God, and the prisoners were listening to them.

Suddenly there was a great earthquake, so that the foundations of the prison were shaken; and immediately all the doors were opened and everyone's chains were loosed. And the keeper of the prison, awaking from sleep and seeing the prison doors open, supposing the prisoners had fled, drew his sword and was about to kill himself. But Paul called with a loud voice, saying, "Do yourself no harm, for we are all here." Then he called for a light, ran in, and fell down trembling before Paul and Silas.

And he brought them out and said, "Sirs, what must I do to be saved?" So, they said, "Believe on the Lord Jesus Christ, and you will be saved, you and your household." Then they spoke the word of the Lord to him and to all who were in his house. And he took them the same hour of the night and washed their stripes. And immediately he and all his family were baptized. Now when he had brought them into his house, he set food before them; and he rejoiced, having believed in God with all his household." - **Acts 16:22-34 NKJV**

It was their complete trust in God (so much so that they could still worship God though everything looked bleak in the natural) that turned their situation around, and not only had them released, but bore the fruit of salvation for the jailer and his household.

Likewise, when we can worship and delight ourselves in God, no matter how the situation looks, or how many prayers we've offered, or how long we have waited for those prayers to be answered, He will give you the desires of your heart. It's firmly promised in the Bible and God is not a man that He should lie!

> *"God is not a man, that He should lie, nor a son of man, that He should repent. Has He said, and will He not do? Or has He spoken, and will He not make it good?"* – **Numbers 23:19 NKJV**

If you are sure that God's answer is "Yes!", then no matter what the circumstance looks like, you can have the assurance of faith, for He is faithful. Therefore, you can give Him your worship and thanksgiving as you delight yourself in Him. There may be delays, testings, or preparation periods, but He WILL do as He has said!!

Whose Faith Does God Respond to?

In your mind you may be still questioning what happens in the prayer line. Whose faith does God respond to before we see a miracle happen? Is it the pray-er's responsibility to have faith, or the one being prayed for? Is it the congregation's faith? How does that work? Is it all three? Is it the gift of faith, or perhaps a special gift of healing that's in operation? Who is responsible to have faith?

Before we discuss examples of "whose faith", I want to make a further distinction between faith and lack of faith. Jesus really got upset with people's lack of faith when He arrived back down the mountain of transfiguration. Let's take a look at the story and see what was really going on there.

> *"And when they had come to the multitude, a man came to Him, kneeling down to Him and saying, 'Lord, have mercy on my son, for he is an epileptic and suffers severely; for he often falls into the fire and often into the water. So, I brought him to Your disciples, but they could not cure him.'*

Then Jesus answered and said, "O ***faithless and perverse generation****, how long shall I be with you? How long shall I bear with you? Bring him here to Me."*

And Jesus rebuked the demon, and it came out of him; and the child was cured from that very hour.

Then the disciples came to Jesus privately and said, "Why could we not cast it out?"

So, Jesus said to them, 'Because of your unbelief; for assuredly, I say to you, if you have faith as a mustard seed, you will say to this mountain, 'Move from here to there,' and it will move; and nothing will be impossible for you. However, this kind does not go out except by prayer and fasting.'" – **Matthew 17:14-21 NKJV**

While Jesus was up the mountain, a man with an epileptic son had gone to Jesus' disciples wanting them to heal his son. This man's faith was in those who would pray for His son, and not God (otherwise healing would have manifested in response to his faith, but it didn't manifest!)

Likewise, the disciples were trying to heal in their own strength. How do I know this? Because nothing happened and Jesus berates them for lacking in faith. (In mark 9:14-29, which reports on the same event, the man asks Jesus if He can do anything, to have compassion on him and his son. Jesus replies, "*If?!*" Actually, what He said was, "*If you can believe, all things are possible to him who believes.*" The man then said that he believed but asked Jesus to help his unbelief. (Perhaps he wasn't fully convinced, especially after the disciples failed.) The man did not have his eyes on the one who really has the power to heal.

The disciples then wanted to know why *they* couldn't heal

the boy. But Jesus tells them it's not their confidence in themselves, nor the amount of faith they had. It only takes a mustard seed sized faith in the One who does the healing miracle, to see it manifest. How much did they trust God to heal this boy. Was it a too big an "ask" for them?

This happens all the time. Have you heard people say, "*Lord send me someone with a headache to heal, not a paralytic in a wheelchair!*" To them at that time, they saw the problem as too big for them to solve rather than God. Whatever their problem, they obviously had misplaced faith, for God is the God of the impossible.

Nevertheless, Jesus went on to tell the disciples that this particular demon was stubborn. Showing one's badge of authority by saying, "*...in Jesus' name...*" is not enough to convince the demon he must go. We need the dunamis power of the Holy Spirit, and His wisdom and guidance to know how best to deal with certain spirits.

Let me give you an illustration that my old pastor (Ps Tony Smits) gave to his students. It's like a policeman directing traffic. He wears the uniform and the badge of authority, so most drivers obey his command. However, not everyone wants to be obedient to this badged man in uniform. There are thugs that would happily plant the foot on the accelerator and plough on through the intersection, whether they were told to stop or not. Nevertheless, if that same policeman was really superman in disguise (that is, with the dunamis power of the Holy Spirit backing him up), he could reach out to that rebellious driver's car, grab the bonnet and shout, "*I said stop!*" and the car would be brought to an abrupt halt. Likewise, this particular demon was stubborn, and required the help of the Holy Spirit to force the issue. This is why the disciples also failed.

However, the point of the entire discourse, is not about the demon and casting out demons, but that all concerned lacked faith in God! Their eyes were not on the One who could heal, otherwise healing would have been readily available.

Okay. These things can happen in a prayer line, but whose faith does God respond to? I would say that God simply responds to faith. Period! It doesn't matter whose. Where there is faith in Him, He is moved to respond. And we can find examples in the Bible of each. God responds when only **one single person has faith**. How does that work?

It could be the one asking for prayer or the one who is praying for the miracle on their behalf. So, let's start with and example those asking, by considering the woman with the issue of blood (Matt 9:20-22).

> "*And suddenly, a woman who had a flow of blood for twelve years came from behind and touched the hem of His garment. For she said to herself, "If only I may touch His garment, I shall be made well." But Jesus turned around, and when He saw her, He said, "Be of good cheer, daughter; your faith has made you well." And the woman was made well from that hour.*" - **Matthew 9:20-22 NKJV**

This was her last hope. She was an unclean outcast. She had to keep away, but she knew that He was powerful in God – the Messiah. Therefore, she only really needed to touch the fringe of His garment (possibly His prayer shawl). The tassels (tzitzit) on each corner of a prayer shawl are attached through the scripture verses that are embroidered on patches on each corner. In an article by scholar Yehuda Shurpin he explains their significance:

"Rabbi Shlomo Yitzchaki (Rashi) quotes a teaching that the corners of the tallit are alluded to in a verse describing the Exodus: "I carried you on the wings of eagles." (Exodus 19:4) The word "kanaf", or "wing," can also mean "corner." As for why there are specifically four corners, Rashi goes on to explain that they correspond to the four expressions of redemption associated with the Exodus: ***"I will take you out . . . I will save you . . . I will redeem you . . . I will take you*** *. . ."* (Exodus 6:6-7)"[3]

There is much more that can be said on this but I feel it is off topic. The fact is, this woman just wanted to touch the fringes, the tzitzits on His garment/shawl. She didn't need long winded public prayers over her. She just needed Him, and the promises of God that He would save her.

There was a crowd pressing around Jesus. Subsequently, no one would even notice her. It was her perfect opportunity. She only needed to grab the tassels – the promises - and receive the healing. This she did, and God's power was released. Not only did she receive healing, but Jesus commended her for her faith (faith not in the tzitzits themselves – they were just a point of contact – but on the power of God manifest in Jesus, His Son, and written as reminders of His promises on the very garments Jesus wore.)

Likewise, blind Bartimaeus outside Jericho (Luke 18:35-43), cried out when he heard that Jesus was passing by. He knew Jesus could heal him and he was determined not to let this moment pass by.

"Then it happened, as He was coming near Jericho,

---

3. Retrieved from the article "Why Must the Tallit have Four Fringed Corners?" by Yehuda Shurpin, and found at https://www.chabad.org/library/article_cdo/aid/2969671/jewish/Why-Must-a-Tallit-Have-Four-Fringed-Corners.htm

> *that a certain blind man sat by the road begging. And hearing a multitude passing by, he asked what it meant. So, they told him that Jesus of Nazareth was passing by. And he cried out, saying, "Jesus, Son of David, have mercy on me!"*
>
> *Then those who went before warned him that he should be quiet; but he cried out all the more, "Son of David,have mercy on me!"So, Jesus stood still and commanded him to be brought to Him. And when he had come near, He asked him, saying, "What do you want Me to do for you?" He said, "Lord, that I may receive my sight."*
>
> *Then Jesus said to him, "Receive your sight;* ***your faith*** *has made you well." And immediately he received his sight, and followed Him, glorifying God. And all the people, when they saw it, gave praise to God."* – **Luke 18:35-43 NKJV**

His conviction, persistence and determination to be healed, delighted Jesus, and he was healed!

Moving on, we know that sometimes miracles happen because of the faith of the one **praying on behalf of another**. Jesus raised the dead on three occasions. It was *His* faith that raised them – obviously it was not the faith of the dead person!

Peter and John's faith healed the lame man as they entered the gate beautiful on their way to temple (Acts 3). The man expected to receive funds, not healing, but the faith of Peter and John healed him.

Consider also those who come **together in agreement** in faith for another (intercessors) – like the paralytic who was let down through the roof in Matthew 9:2 and again in Mark

2:5. The Word says that when Jesus saw *their* faith, He responded. It was the paralytic's friends that were expecting a miracle. Jesus responded to their faith.

Likewise, Jesus also stated that where two or more agree about what they ask the Father for, it will be done for them. (Matthew 18:19) James also instructs the church to call for the elders to anoint and pray for the sick, and that same *prayer of faith* will heal him. (James 5:14)

> "*Is anyone among you sick? Let him call for the elders of the church, and let them pray over him, anointing him with oil in the name of the Lord. And the prayer of faith will save the sick, and the Lord will raise him up.*" - **James 5:14-15 NKJV**

Praying together has power. I was part of a Spirit led intercessory group for many years and can testify that we saw God answer many prayers. It was powerful. That's why we should seek to pray together often – especially as the days grow darker. If you're praying in a group, then you can stand on that promise Jesus gave us, namely:

> "*Again, I say to you that if two of you agree on earth concerning anything that they ask, it will be done for them by My Father in heaven.*" – **Matthew 18:19 NKJV**

Sometimes, however, it's a **God ordained moment** when the Holy Spirit intervenes. Just like when Jesus raised the dead man because He had compassion on the young man's mother (Luke 7:12-15) who was weeping as the funeral procession drew near.

> "*And when He came near the gate of the city, behold, a dead man was being carried out, the only son of his mother; and she was a widow. And a large crowd from*

> *the city was with her. When the Lord saw her, He had compassion on her and said to her, "Do not weep." Then He came and touched the open coffin, and those who carried him stood still. And He said, "Young man, I say to you, arise." So, he who was dead sat up and began to speak. And He presented him to his mother."* - **Luke 7:12-15 NKJV**

Likewise, God may give us a compassion to pray, or the gift of faith. It's like a sudden, "You just know, that you know, that you know that God's got this. It's a given! It will happen!" When God wants it done, He empowers us to trust Him. We obey and it just happens by the power of the Holy Spirit. There's no time for trying to talk yourself into believing, or having enough faith. You just know it's God's leading and that He will make it happen, and He does. All the glory is completely His!!

As I've already discussed, in any of these cases, it's not the *amount* of faith we have, but that we have faith in the One who is able to do the impossible, because we know Him and His character personally. Our eyes are fixed on Him alone, and not on our performance or worthiness, or merely in the act of receiving and/or our preparedness to receive, nor how much faith we happened to have, or the faith of the person praying for us. Our faith is squarely in God who is both able to do the impossible, and who is the absolute top of the chain of command. What He says, goes! It's a sure thing!

Chapter 2

Hearing God's Voice with Clarity

~~~~~~~~~~~~~~

One of the big roadblocks to obtaining the desired answers to prayer is misunderstanding, or the misinterpreting, what God is saying and/or promising us. This can result in misplaced faith. Then, when it fails, we're left confused; wondering why God would let us down. This further leads to disappointment, despondency, and doubt - as I have already discussed. What we really need is clarity and certainty.

For example, you may be asking God for something in the "*not promised in the Bible*" category, and be unsure if it is in His will or not. Unfortunately, sometimes the desire for the particular outcome can be louder than our ability to hear God whisper His will to us. It's like looking through a filter. If I look through a red filter, everything appears red. If I look through a blue filter, everything appears blue. Likewise, if I look through the filter of my desires – things I've not only been thinking about over and over but have an emotional longing for – everything we see or hear will be seen through that lens. Whereas in past times we would not have noticed certain "signs", suddenly they loom larger than life, because they are related to those things on our mind or in our heart. As a result, we can mistake those things as some kind of confirmation of our request, but in reality, they may not be.

Even other people who say they are prophetic may not hear accurately, and this false prophecy may even send us in a completely wrong direction. Subsequently, we need a better way to hear God's heart on the matter.
~~~~~~~~~~~~~~

Having said that, I'd like to digress a little with this topic so that you are fully equipped, able to hear God with clarity, and therefore, able to stand in faith, knowing that the One who is able, has or has not granted your request.

Hearing Our Good Shepherd

OK. How do we hear God for ourselves? Let me state up front that Jesus said that His sheep would hear His voice.

> "*But he who enters by the door is the shepherd of the sheep. To him the doorkeeper opens, and the sheep hear his voice; and he calls his own sheep by name and leads them out. And when he brings out his own sheep, he goes before them; and the sheep follow him, for they know his voice. Yet they will by no means follow a stranger, but will flee from him, for they do not know the voice of strangers.*" - **John 10:1-5 NKJV**

> "*I am the good shepherd; and I know My sheep, and am known by My own. As the Father knows Me, even so I know the Father; and I lay down My life for the sheep. And other sheep I have which are not of this fold; them also I must bring, and they will* ***hear My voice****; and there will be one flock and one shepherd.*" - **John 10: 14-16 NKJV**

> "*My sheep* ***hear My voice****, and I know them, and they follow Me*" – **John 10:27 NKJV**

If you are one of His sheep – His follower – you will know His voice. However, although many believers have always instinctively known when has God spoken to them, others simply do not know, nor do they have a grip on how this can be achieved. Why? Possibly because they have never really been taught. Often, those that could hear our Good

Shepherd's voice assumed others should too, but that's not always the case.

Dr Mark Virkler, author of, "*Four Keys to Hearing God's Voice*"[4], was one of those people, until he realised that others could not hear God speak to them. He then set out a step-by-step approach to teach people how to hear God's voice. I absolutely recommend you reading his book if you are lacking in this area, because he not only gives you the practical steps but shows you by Scripture verse, why and how we should do these things.

Natural, in his book, Dr. Mark Virkler does a much better job than me in discussing this and has many practical exercises for you to try. I strongly suggest you grab a copy for yourself.

Nevertheless, the steps Dr Mark Virkler suggests are:

> 1) **Quiet yourself down** and be still in His presence. This might take some practice, but I have personally found that my mind is the quietest first thing in the morning.
>
> 2) **Fix your eyes and attention completely upon Jesus**. Before I start listening, I normally do my Bible study. That helps me to immensely, as I am already tuned in and listening to the Holy Spirit through the Scriptures. Other people like to pray in tongues or have some worship music playing quietly in the background. Although the new age movement has plenty of counterfeits in this area, using your sanctified imagination as God intended, will help you.

---

4. "*4 Keys to Hearing God's Voice*" copyright 2010 Mark & Patty Virkler, produced by Destiny Image Publishers Inc. Also available at www.CWGMinistries.org.

See yourself at the feet of Jesus, like Mary of Bethany, or walking with Him in one of the gospel stories.

3) **Listen for, and recognise God's voice** in your heart and tune in to what He is saying. (See more on this below) It will appear as a spontaneous thought, or image, or sensation. Keep listening/watching.

4) **Write down what God tells/shows you.** This is important for submitting to others who are far more skilled and competent in this area, and who discern whether you are actually hearing from God or not. Plus, it's handy for your own records, should you need to revisit the things God reveals to you.

Of course, as well as our own voice, there are other spiritual voices we need to be able to differentiate between if we are to know with certainty what God is speaking to us. The hard truth is that the enemy can whisper things to us as well. So, how can we possibly tell the difference? Are there Biblical guidelines to help? The answer is "Yes!", there are in fact, five major precautions you can take, to ensure you filter out the lies. These are particularly important as you first start your journey. As you become more confident, you will know that you know, but when setting out, these tests are imperative. They are:

1) **Test the origins of the voice** (1 John 4:1). One big tell if it's your own voice is that our own minds tend to follow a line of progressive thoughts. One thought leads to another and so on. However, when God speaks to us, it can appear spontaneously. Dr Mark Virkler adds,

> "*The Hebrew word for true prophecy is* ***naba****, which literally means to bubble up, whereas false prophecy*

*is **ziyd** meaning to boil up. True words from the Lord will bubble up from our innermost being; we don't need to cook them up ourselves.*"

2) Does it conflict with the Bible or the principles it upholds? God will never contradict His Word (the Scriptures) or the truths it contains! Sin is still sin and He will not say otherwise. Therefore, this implies that you study the Word to know the truth.

3) Does it contradict the character of God? What God utters will be in complete harmony with His character, especially as described in the very names of the Father, Son and Holy Spirit.

4) Test the fruit (Matthew 7:15-20). When you hear the word, how does that make you feel in your spirit man? Is there a quickening in your faith, and an increase in your love, peace and joy? OR, do these words cause fear, doubt, confusion, anxiety, or even bolster up your ego.

5) Share it with your spiritual advisers. This assumes, of course, that your spiritual advisors are people who are trustworthy, know the word of God, and are known to hear God accurately. Although you don't need the top prophet available, (simply people you know can hear God and in whom you trust), they should not be self-proclaimed car-park-only prophets, or self-proclaimed authorities either.

Proverbs states,

"*Where there is no counsel, the people fall; But in the multitude of counsellors there is safety.*" - **Proverbs 11:14 NKJV**

We are a body with members. We work together for the good of the body. This is how we grow as individuals and as a church.

This discussion has been centred around the very foundations to hearing God supernaturally, but there are layers to the prophetic and prophetic giftings that I now wish to discuss so that there is no confusion.

Three Groups of Gifts

God has given us different types, or groups, of gifts, but all given so that we can serve one another with them. Note: they are not for our own benefit but for the edification, and encouragement of your brethren, for building up, for direction and guidance, and for serving one another.

> "*God has given each of you a gift from his great variety of spiritual gifts. Use them well to serve one another.*"
> – **1 Peter 4:10 NLT**

Paul too, in speaking about unity despite differences in abilities and ministries states that there are different gifts given by each person of the God head but still only one body, one hope, one faith, one baptism, and each gift is given in the measure God decides.

> "*'There is one body and one **Spirit**, just as you were called in one hope of your calling; one **Lord**, one faith, one baptism; one God and **Father** of all, who is above all, and through all, and in you all. But to each one of us grace was given according to the measure of Christ's gift.*" - **Ephesians 4:4-7 NKJV**

That is, the group of gifts that each person of the Trinty gives, differs in purpose to the other groups, but all function together for the good of the whole.

a) There are **Spiritual gifts** of which there are nine.

> "*A spiritual gift is given to each of us so we can help each other. To one person the Spirit gives the ability to give* ***wise advice;*** *to another the same Spirit gives a message of* ***special knowledge****. The same Spirit gives* ***great faith*** *to another, and to someone else the one Spirit gives the* ***gift of healing****. He gives one person the* ***power to perform miracles****, and another the* ***ability to prophesy****. He gives someone else the* ***ability to discern*** *whether a message is from the Spirit of God or from another spirit. Still another person is given the ability to* ***speak in unknown languages****, while another is given the* ***ability to interpret*** *what is being said. It is the one and only Spirit who distributes all these gifts. He alone decides which gift each person should have.*"
> **– 1 Corinthians 12:7-11 NLT**

b) There are gifts that **Christ**, Himself, gives to the church. That is, the fivefold ministries.

> "*Now these are the gifts Christ gave to the church: the* ***apostles****, the* ***prophets****, the* ***evangelists****, and the* ***pastors*** *and* ***teachers****. Their responsibility is to equip God's people to do his work and build up the church, the body of Christ.*" – **Ephesians 4:11-12 NKJV**

c) Lastly, there are gifts given to each person by the **Father**. These are known as the motivational gifts.

> "*For as we have many members in one body, but all the members do not have the same function, so we, being many, are one body in Christ, and individually members of one another. Having then gifts differing ac-*

cording to the grace that is given to us, let us use them: if prophecy, let us prophesy in proportion to our faith; or ***ministry*** *(another word for service), let us use it in our ministering; he who* ***teaches****, in teaching; he who* ***exhorts****, in exhortation; he who* ***gives****, with liberality; he who* ***leads****, with diligence; he who* ***shows mercy****, with cheerfulness.*" - **Romans 12:4-8 NKJV**

These are grace gifts, given to us without merit, and to all men. When each of us are conceived, we are all given one or more motivational gifts. These help to shape our personalities and our ultimate vocation in life. Everyone has a motivational gifting.

(This is by no means a new teaching. Many have written books about the various gifts. One that I particularly would recommend for the motivational gifts is "*Discover Your God Given Gifts*" by Don & Katie Fortune[5]. It has an excellent explanation of the gifts. (The Fortunes have even given test sheets in their book for you to discover your own strengths. You may have a couple of gifts which rank highly that interact with one another.)

Finally, Paul gives a brief condensed list of all three categories *working together* in the church, in 1 Corinthians 12:

"*And God has appointed these in the church: first* ***apostles****, second* ***prophets****, third teachers, after that,* ***miracles****, then gifts of* ***healings, helps, administrations, varieties of tongues****. Are all apostles? Are all prophets? Are all teachers? Are all workers of miracles?*

---

5 "Discover Your God Given Gifts" by Don & Katie Fortune, copyright © 1987 Don & Katie Fortune, Published by Chosen Books a division of Baker Publishing Group P.O. Box 6287, Grand Rapids, MI 49516-6287 www.chosenbooks.com

Do all have gifts of healings? Do all speak with tongues? Do all interpret?" – **1 Corinthians 12:28-30 NKJV**

That is: the Ministry gifts of Apostles, Prophets, Teachers, the Spiritual gifts of Miracles, healings, tongues, interpretation of tongues, and the Motivational gifts of Helps/servers, administrations.

The Gifts in Detail

The Motivational/Grace Gifts

These gifts are given to us without merit and by the Father and as such are also known as grace gifts. As already quoted above, Paul explains how they work together within the body of Christ. Here is that verse again for you:

> "*For as we have many members in one body, but all the members do not have the same function, so we, being many, are one body in Christ, and individually members of one another. Having then gifts differing according to the grace that is given to us, let us use them: if **prophecy**, let us prophesy in proportion to our faith; or **ministry** (another word for service), let us use it in our ministering; he who **teaches**, in teaching; he who exhorts, in **exhortation**; he who **gives**, with liberality; he who **leads**, with diligence; he who **shows mercy**, with cheerfulness.*" - **Romans 12:4-8 NKJV**

When each of us are conceived, we are all given one or more motivational gifts. These may have some part to play in shaping our personalities (though a person's personality can be altered by their experiences in life, their choices, and their values), but more importantly, they direct us to our ultimate vocation in life. (Note: testing for these gifts is **not** like doing a personality test like Myers-Briggs Type

Indicator (MBTI), Minnesota Multiphasic Personality Inventory (MMPI), or Big Five Personality Test, or some other personality indicator test. These motivational gifts are given to us by God for the purposes of the Kingdom, and in some way direct us to our calling. That is because we are thus gifted, we gravitate towards things we are "good at", and therefore, to our God-given destiny in life.) God designed our lives before we came to be. He had a plan and purpose for our lives in mind!

> "*For You formed my innermost parts; You knit me [together] in my mother's womb. I will give thanks and praise to You, for I am fearfully and wonderfully made; Wonderful are Your works, and my soul knows it very well. My frame was not hidden from You, When I was being formed in secret, and intricately and skilfully formed [as if embroidered with many colours] in the depths of the earth. Your eyes have seen my unformed substance; And in Your book were all written the days that were appointed for me, when as yet there was not one of them [even taking shape].*"
> – **Psalm 139: 13-16 AMP**

If God so meticulously planned our physical bodies, it doesn't take much to realise that He planned our giftedness. Just as our DNA determines and brings forth our physical characteristics, the Fortunes explain, "*so our motivational gifts bring forth the interests, abilities, enthusiasms, and actions that make us effective members of the body of Christ.*" The Fortunes go on in their book (*Discover Your God Given Gifts*) to explain why they came to the conclusion that these gifts were given at birth.

The thing that convinced the Fortunes of this was their studies with identical twins who were separated at birth and never knew each other. So many correlations between the twins having exactly the same gifts, that it was hard to ignore. (You can read about them in their book.) However, upon later reading about a pair of twins in an article in the Reader's Digest they were pretty much convinced. Here is the exert:

> *'Identical twin boys, born in Ohio some 40 years ago, were adopted by different families shortly after birth. A year ago, after 39 years apart, they were reunited. It was discovered that each had been named James; that each had had law-enforcement training; that each liked mechanical drawing and carpentry. Each married a woman named Linda, had a son—one named James Alan and the other James Allan—had divorced, and then married a second wife named Betty. Both had dogs named Toy. Also, both favoured the same St. Petersburg, Florida, vacation beach'.*[6]

These twins were raised apart in very different families, and lived far enough away from one another that there was no possibility they or their families could ever meet, yet the similarities were striking, and there had to be more to it than mere DNA. At conception, God gives no just the physical characteristics, but the spiritual ones too.

That being said, since we are gifted at conception, a person can ultimately use their gift for kingdom service when they are saved, but an unsaved person can equally use it for employment or activities of their own. (For example, people with a dual teacher/perceiver gifting set may become barristers where the teaching gift facilitates the digging for information and truth, and the perception gift to follow

---

6. Edward Ziegler, "*The Mysterious Bonds of Twins*," The Reader's Digest (January 1980): p. 78.

"hunches" and leads. Compassion gifted people may become counsellors, and administrators, CEO's. There are far more details and descriptions in the book named below, and years of studies where people have been interviewed and data found to back this statement up.)

When you stop to consider these differences, it makes for a very harmonious and interconnected society. It simply wouldn't work so well, if everyone wanted to do the same vocation/job in life. Who would then do the rest of the jobs required to run a society in a cohesive manner? For example, not everyone can nor wants to be a doctor, or a plumber, or a pilot. What would society look like if that were the case, and how could it possibly function? People have different preferences in their jobs in life. Paul makes this very point when he speaks about all the members being needed for the body of Christ to function. (Romans 12:12-27) Indeed, God in His great wisdom, even made provision for this!

How does this work? When a person with the motivational gift of prophecy/perception matures and is saved, they will gravitate or be drawn towards the spiritual gift of prophecy, and earnestly seek it. Conversely, the unsaved may be drawn to clairvoyancy and even the occult. (This is by no means a new teaching.) Nevertheless, God intended that each one of use would use our gifts not just to enable society to function smoothly, but for the benefit of the kingdom as a whole. If we have a certain gift, we should therefore, use it for His purposes, and to serve one another. Therefore, Peter aptly says,

> "*As each one has received a gift, minister it to one another, as good stewards of the manifold grace of God.*"- **1Peter 4:10 NKJV**

Note: Everyone has at least one major grace gift, but they also usually have a degree (large or minute) of all the motivational giftings. Jesus was an all-rounder – able to do all things well. You may even have a couple of gifts which rank highly that interact with one another.

The Spiritual Gifts

> *"A spiritual gift is given to each of us so we can help each other. To one person the Spirit gives: the ability to give* ***wise advice****; to another the same Spirit gives a message of* ***special knowledge****. The same Spirit gives* ***great faith*** *to another, and to someone else the one Spirit gives the gift of* ***healing****. He gives one person the power to* ***perform miracles****, and another the ability to* ***prophesy****. He gives someone else the ability to* ***discern*** *whether a message is from the Spirit of God or from another spirit. Still another person is given the ability to* ***speak in unknown languages****, while another is given the ability to* ***interpret*** *what is being said. It is the one and only Spirit who distributes all these gifts. He alone decides which gift each person should have."*
> **– 1 Corinthians 12:7-11 NLT**

The Spiritual gifts are for the edification of the body and for building the kingdom. They operate with the church, and often accompany evangelists and those preaching the gospel, bringing to life the further credence of the Kingdom message to unbelievers. Having these gifts does not mean we have attained some level of holiness, or that we are above our brethren. These are gifts/tools for God's use, and will pass away once we enter heaven.

> *"Love never fails. But where there are prophecies, they will cease; where there are tongues, they will be stilled; where there is knowledge, it will pass away. For we*

> *know in part and we prophesy in part, but when completeness comes, what is in part disappears. When I was a child, I talked like a child, I thought like a child, I reasoned like a child. When I became a man, I put the ways of childhood behind me. For now we see only a reflection as in a mirror; then we shall see face to face. Now I know in part; then I shall know fully, even as I am fully known. And now these three remain: faith, hope and love. But the greatest of these is love."* – **1 Corinthians 13:8-13 NIV**

Nevertheless, previously to stating this, Paul tells us to earnestly desire the **Spiritual gifts**:

> *"But earnestly desire the best/higher/greater gifts. And yet I show you a more excellent way."* – **1 Corinthians 12:31 NKJV**

(He then goes on to speak about love being the ultimate ability in 1 Corinthians 13.) We also know that the children of God can pray and the Father who will gladly give the Holy Spirit and gifts to those who ask:

> *"So, I say to you, ask, and it will be given to you; seek, and you will find; knock, and it will be opened to you. For everyone who asks receives, and he who seeks finds, and to him who knocks it will be opened. If a son asks for bread from any father among you, will he give him a stone? Or if he asks for a fish, will he give him a serpent instead of a fish? Or if he asks for an egg, will he offer him a scorpion? If you then, being evil, know how to give good gifts to your children,* ***how much more will your heavenly Father give the Holy Spirit to those who ask Him!****"* – **Luke 11:9-13 NKJV**

Therefore, even if we do not have a related motivational

gift, we can still **ask in faith** for a spiritual gift and it will be granted to us, so long as we earnestly desire it. Roughly speaking there are three groups of gifts:

1. **Revelation-gifts**

    * Word of wisdom

    * Word of knowledge

    * Discerning of spirits

2. **Power-gifts**

    * Faith

    * Gifts of healings

    * Working of miracles

3. **Speaking/vocal-gifts**

    * Speaking in tongues

    * Interpretation

    * Prophecy

These can also be given permanently, or temporarily for a particular incident/occasion – the Holy Spirit working through you simply because you're the only one around at the time, (for example the gift of faith, or the gift of healing). When given permanently, they are for you to minister to your brethren, and for the overall local church's edification. Once given for permanent use, they are not rescinded, even if you go off the rails.

> *"For the gifts and the calling of God are irrevocable."* - **Romans 11:29 NKJV**

This means that if you once had the gift of prophecy, even if you have turned your back on Christ, you may still hear spiritually, but it may no longer be the Holy Spirit that you hear, but rather an unholy one! Therefore, it is important to know the voice of God and to stay on track in your relationship with Him.

The Fivefold Ministries

> *"Now these are the gifts Christ gave to the church: the **apostles**, the **prophets**, the **evangelists**, and the **pastors** and **teachers**. Their responsibility is to equip God's people to do his work and build up the church, the body of Christ."* – **Ephesians 4:11-12 NKJV**

The last group is **fivefold** ministries/ministers which are gifts Christ gives to the church. These are appointed by Christ, but also recognised by the church oversight/leadership as being apparent in a person's Christian life. They will not just be "good at what they do", and carry a strong anointing in that area, but they will have a strong desire to *train up others*, i.e., to equip the saints for the work of ministry. We find the supporting Scripture in Ephesians. Paul writes:

> *"And He Himself gave some to be apostles, some prophets, some evangelists, and some pastors and teachers, for the equipping of the saints for the work of ministry, for the edifying of the body of Christ"* – **Ephesians 4:11-12 NKJV**

Let's take a closer look at the function of each of these fivefold ministries, and discuss how these differ from the

Spiritual and motivational gifts and how the three groups of gifts might support one another.

* Although the head of the local church is labelled the pastor or senior pastor, this term usually refers to the head shepherd of the flock. However, the pastor of a church need not necessarily be a **fivefold pastor**. He could equally be an apostle, a teacher, or some other five-fold minister, or perhaps operate in a couple of these ministry giftings – at least until they can recognise other five-fold ministers that Jesus has placed and appointed within their church to assist in the work there.

Generally speaking, fivefold pastors will have a nurturing spirit that attracts many. People feel like they can trust/talk to them, so they often head up the counselling team at the church. Their number one motivational gifting is usually compassion/mercy. Their thrust is always caring for the flock, and seeing that spiritual needs are meet in Christ Jesus, that is, always pointing to Jesus as the answer that people are seeking. Thus, five-fold pastors also have a strong desire to start care groups where they will train up carers and counsellors to deal with people's problems and visit congregants, and so on.

* **Fivefold prophets** will have an accuracy and weight/authority in the prophetic. Many of them will also be able to declare a thing and see it happen. They normally help bring direction & even correction to the local church, and work alongside the headship to ensure the church moves in line with the directions of the Holy Spirit. Although they often prophesy over the church, they can also give individual prophecies within the local church, though

this may not be frequent. Five-fold prophets also desire to train up people in the prophetic so that confusion can be eradicated, and the next generation of prophets can operate accurately within the local church.

* **Fivefold teachers** carry a revelatory spirit with regard to the Word of God and the mysteries it contains. They are also able to articulate and explain these precepts of God both in a manner that people understand, and that conveys the revelation accurately and without ambiguity. They <u>don't</u> usually teach "*how to teach*". Their mandate is to pass the revelations of God to others.

As such, they have an inbuilt strong desire to teach God's word, and encourage people to read and study their Bibles for themselves, even giving out constant tips on the best/most effective ways this can be achieved. Simply put, fivefold teachers teach believers the word of God, training the people up in truth, so as to sharpen their swords, ready to cut down any lies. They desire all brethren walk in absolute Biblical truth and knowledge so as not to be deceived. In fact, teachers hate lies or deceptive Biblical interpretations! They can be quite pedantic when faced with doctrinal errors and misinterpretation of Scriptures.

The natural progression of this fivefold gift may also manifest in the desire to disciple younger Christians in Biblical foundational truths, and/or create special Bible study groups where students dig even deeper into the word of God. Some may even choose to work in a Bible School environment where they can fully utilise their gift.

This gift may have started as a grace/motivational gift (i.e. a person has always had a teaching/instructing "bent" in their life), but the Holy Spirit equipped them further with anointed revelation, until such time as their gift was recognised, (by the church) as being Spirit filled, anointed, and God ordained.

* **Fivefold evangelists** have a special anointing for evangelism, and they easily win souls to Christ. For them it is very natural to approach a stranger and begin a Christ filled conversation. They seem to easily converse, and spiritually persuade the lost to take a look at Jesus as the answer for their lives. This is their anointing. At the same time, because of their hunger for souls, they have a desire to see the body of Christ witnessing as well, and to this end train up other people to do this well.

* And finally, **fivefold apostles** have a strong anointing for building and growing churches. Their strongly desire to see the kingdom culture – the culture of heaven – maintained within the church. Remember that ships known as "apostle-ships" were first sent out by the Romans to bring the culture of Rome to the lands they had conquered. Thus, Jesus' apostles were to bring the culture of heaven to all those they encountered. This meant healing the sick, evangelising and preaching the kingdom, teaching, caring for the flock, and operating in the prophetic. As well as being good all-rounders in the other four five-fold ministries (though obviously not to the same level), they have very good administrative/co-ordinating skills for managing the flock and raising up the next generation of leaders. Anyone they recognise with leadership potential, they will guide/train to be better leaders and may even sug-

gest they attend Bible college, or some other sort of ministry training.

As this discussion details, **the functions of each of the groups of gifts are different**. Simply put, just because a person can hear God's voice, they are not suddenly a five-fold prophet. There is process, training and calling, and finally appointment.

Finally, these three groups of gifts all work together for the benefit of the body of Christ as a whole. Remember Paul gave a brief condensed list of all three categories working together, in 1 Corinthians 12:

> "*And God has appointed these in the church: first **apostles**, second **prophets**, third teachers, after that, **miracles**, then gifts of **healings, helps, administrations, varieties of tongues**. Are all apostles? Are all prophets? Are all teachers? Are all workers of miracles? Do all have gifts of healings? Do all speak with tongues? Do all interpret?*" – **1 Corinthians 12:28-30 NKJV**

As mentioned, in these verses, Paul gives a brief summary of all the gifts that should be operating and functioning together within the church. These all work together for the perfect function and coordination of the local church, and we see this (or should) regularly each Sunday, and whenever the church meets together.

Hearing God Through the Prophetic

Prophecy as a motivational gift enables you to hear and discern clearly on a personal level. We should all hear our Good Shepherds voice, but there are **three other distinct functions** of the *prophetic gifts*.

1) The ability to "know" or discern on a personal level in a prophetic manner comes via the ***motivational gifts***.

2) The Holy Spirit also has a ***gift of prophecy*** that enables a person to "hear/see" and proclaim prophetic utterances over people and the local church.

3) The ***Office of a Prophe***t (5-fold minister) is a ministry that Jesus, Himself assigns to the church, to not only bring direction and correction to the local church, but to teach others with clarity and understandably, how to operate in this gift (i.e. they can equip the saints in this area of ministry which will minimize cowboy prophets arising and thus, confusing the church.)

Those that have that inbuilt ability in sensing/hearing in the supernatural (i.e. the motivational gift of perception/prophecy, or "*Perceivers*" as the Fortunes have labelled them) have been given this gift by God, the Father, and have had it from conception. It's something they have always been able to hear.

For example: I am a perceiver/teacher. (I tested well above 90% on both gifts.) I've always had the ability to know certain things: Sometimes I could hear a person's words before they spoke. Sometimes I knew/sensed something about a particular person. Sometimes I knew events well before they happened, and this was all *before I was saved*. I was born with that ability.

My first major encounter really with the prophetic occurred when I was still very young and not saved. I was about 5 years old, (though I may have been much younger), when an old water main pipe that was buried relatively close to the surface of the ground in our back yard, burst outside my bedroom window during the night. It sounded like a waterfall as the water gushed out with mains force pressure, flooding our whole yard (parts were quite deep in fact) and the street beyond.

I emerged blurry eyed from my room to see mum and dad running here and there trying to reach people on the emergency number at the Water Board, and to have the water turned off before the house floated away. I was made to go back to bed and a few hours later the problem was resolved. The following next few days, workmen pumped water from the property and fixed the pipes, but this is far from the end of the tale!

A few months later, after the land had been dried out and the mains water pipe fixed, I was again woken in the middle of the night to the same watery sound. I looked out of my window peering into the darkness, and saw flooding water covering the entire back yard as before. The strange thing was, this time no one else was out of bed attending to the problem. This can't be! Don't they know what's happening! I ran into my parents' bedroom and woke them with the news. Dad hurriedly donned his robe and went to check the damage.

There was nothing! Not a drop! I protested and told them I had heard it and saw it from my window. I was insistent and wouldn't take "No" for an answer. I knew what I had seen and heard! Dad would argue no further. He simply told mum to put me to bed and to shine a torch from my window into the backyard to show me otherwise. To my astonishment and my insistence that it was not what I saw, the yard was completely dry. When she had convinced me that I must have been dreaming, I was put back to bed.

The next night however, I was woken again by the same sound. Again, I checked outside my window only to see what I had seen the night before. Again, I went and woke my parents. Unfortunately, this time with my parent's discovery of no broken mains water pipe or flooding in the yard, I was sent back to bed with a warning that if I ever woke them up again in the middle of the night, there better be a major flood or I would be wearing a sore behind!

Finally on the third night, I woke again to the same sound. I listened hard for some time to make sure I wasn't simply imagining things. I peered into the darkness from my window, blinking, squinting, and straining my eyes to be sure. It was definitely there, and yes, I could hear the water. This was no dream or object of my imagination.

Being too afraid of my dad, I decided I was not going to wake my parents, and instead woke my brother Neil, so that he could confirm what I was seeing and he could tell dad. My brother ran straight to the front door and opened it only to see the water lapping at his feet. This time, there was water everywhere. Needless to say, my parents didn't scold me, but quickly took action. Dad then also alerted our neighbours whose firewood had started to float down to the creek. In fact, this event became the topic of conversation in the weeks to follow, with our neighbour claiming that I had saved their house. Really it was God. He had warned me prophetically, saving not just me but all of us!

How can I put a label on this? It wasn't the Holy Spirit Gift of Prophecy – I wasn't even saved! It was definitely not five-fold. I was far too young for any of that. Obviously, I had been given the grace gift of perception, with an ability to hear. (Like a brand-new car waiting to be filled with the good oil.) For that particular occasion the Holy Spirit was able to supply what was needed for that one time, in order to protect us all. However, that didn't mean I had the Holy Spirit gift of prophecy, but the *potential* to carry it.

Those who are born perceivers will gravitate to the prophetic quite naturally when they are saved. This does not mean that people who are not perceivers can't be prophetic. Paul tells us to pray for the spiritual gift of prophecy.

> "*Pursue love, and desire spiritual gifts, but especially that you may prophesy.*" – **1 Corinthians 14:1 NKJV**

Therefore, if you're not naturally gifted as a perceiver, the Holy Spirit can still empower you. All you need to do if you earnestly desire this gift, is to pray. If you are a perceiver, you can also ask the Holy Spirit for the gift of prophecy so that you can begin not just to hear, but to prophesy! (This, however, does not make you a fivefold prophet! That is a gift that **Jesus appoints** to His church.)

You may start by just hearing God for yourself, then if you are granted the Holy Spirit gift of Prophecy, progress to being able to hear words for others.

The **Holy Spirit Gift of Prophecy** is like the next level. It's sort of obvious, but a person firstly must be saved and filled with the Holy Spirit. When they receive the gift, they begin to hear the word of the Lord for others. Quite often the Vocal Gifts come as a package deal and sometimes are coupled with the Revelation Gifts.

The Vocal Gifts (i.e. Prophecy, tongues and interpretation of tongues) produce **foresight** (for a particular person or for the church). That is, the Holy Spirit reveals where He is taking them or what lies ahead! (e.g. "*It's a new day*", or "*I am raising up people*", or "*I see you doing...*", "*I'm preparing* *you for...*", and so on.) Prophecy gives forewarning, provides encouragement for the future, or even to show possibilities should a person(s) continue to walk a particular path. Prophecy, prophetic tongues and the interpretation of them, are generally for the church and its edification.

However, the vocal gifts can also be used for day-to-day living. For example, tongues are of two categories: prophetic or prayerful. It is the prophetic tongues we often hear in church and they must be accompanied by the interpretation. Prayerful tongues, on the other hand, are for personal edification and personal petitioning of God. In the latter, it is the Holy Spirit who prays through us using prayerful tongues, when we simply do not know how to express the needs, or possibly don't know the full extent of the issues (Rom 8:26). This kind of tongue does not require interpretation.

Prophecy within the church can be for individuals or the church at large. It can operate within prayer lines when God has something in particular that He wants to say or address regarding a person's situation and where that person is headed, and where it is not relevant for the entire church to hear. Within a person's personal life, the gift of prophecy can alert the bearer of the gift to things about to take place and certain preparations/precautions need to take place, or to alert those close to them.

Conversely, the Revelation Gifts (i.e. Wisdom, Knowledge and Discerning of Spirits), offer **insights** - the Holy Spirit is revealing things that are happening within the church of a spiritual nature (e.g. "*God is bringing acceleration...*" or "*God is pouring out healing right now...*" etc.) or things are relevant to individuals who are struggling, or needing direction. These gifts can also alert the leadership of the church about spiritual infiltration, or how to proceed when under intense spiritual pressure (e.g., legal action against the church). As previously mentioned, they often operate side by side with the Vocal Gifts and are sometimes confused since the gifts can work together and boundaries are often blurred.

These Revelation Gifts can, and quite frequently manifest in Spirit led intercession. In this case He is drawing people's attention to further intercede for a particular need or situation, and to reveal things about that issue of which those praying, are unaware. They can also be seen in operation during worship, to alert people to what God is doing or wants to do in a particular time. In a counselling situation too, they have obvious advantages.

The real power of the Revelation Gifts however, can be seen in evangelism, offering yet more validity to the gospel message being preached, and showing individuals that God not only knows about their lives, and has the answer they need.

These people who already have the motivational gift of prophecy/perception, are far more likely to operate in both of these groups of Spiritual Gifts. They are born with the ability to "hear" in the spirit realm. (They were already designed for this.) However, it is not necessarily the case they will operate both the vocal gifts and the revelation gifts, but these gifts often do come as a package deal. (Note: Again, I will say that if you are not a perceiver you can still earnestly desire the Gift of Prophecy, (or any of the Spiritual Gifts) and God will give it/them to you. However, I will include the caveat that these gifts are for God's use and glory!)

A prophetic person may start out by giving personal prophecies, or having dreams and visions relevant to their own lives or others they know. They are for growth, edification and direction. Then, when a person is faithful with their small beginnings and is seeking God for the more, he/she may begin to receive other "words" or prophecies for the church. These may also manifest as dreams and visions, and should always be submitted to the oversight/headship for scrutiny before they are shared with the church at large. Once a prophetic person has proven their "worth", and their prophecies have proven accurate, they may no longer be required submit the messages of the Holy Spirit, but to give them at the appropriate time within the service.

Eventually, if they have a strong desire to train up others, and are seen to be doing so, they may have their gift recognised as ***fivefold***, but it's not automatic. Desiring to be fivefold is not up to the individual persons, whether they undertake to train others or not in order to be seen. It is Christ that gives these gifts to the church. Nor can a person be self-appointed. The gift must be recognised and then appointed by headship. That is that they are not self-appointed, but their gift is recognised and acknowledged by the church/church movement leadership. Their gift is accurate, insightful, and generally aimed at the church rather than individuals. (Not that they can't do both personal and church prophecies, but because of their fivefold office, their function has a different direction than the usual prophets within the church.) They encourage others in their prophetic gifts and teach/train them up in the best ways to use the prophetic gift to encourage others and build up the body of Christ. They also provide heavenly insights into the direction church leaders take and efficient ways to help apostles realign the church to the culture of heaven.

Also, if that person leaves the church and becomes a member of another, the gift is not automatically transferred to the next church. That particular fivefold gift was given to the first church by Christ, Himself. In transferring to another church, you remain prophetic, but it is up to the next church to recognise that gift in operation in you and to discern whether Christ has now provided it for them. God places His order and leaders within each church. Yes, the gifts and callings are irrevocable, and you may have the prophetic gift and calling to operate in the prophetic, but the *office* of fivefold ministry for a particular church is still within the hands of those Jesus Christ places in leadership. That means you can't simply walk into a church and claim you're a fivefold prophet. In that church you're not! You need to submit to the headship there. If you are never recognised as fivefold there, then continue to pray into the situation. Allow God to open people's eyes to your gift, and then also allow Him to appoint as He sees fit.

Finally, there are fivefold prophets that are released to the greater global body of Christ, (people like John Paul Jackson when he was still alive, Bob Jones, Cindy Jacobs and others). These are able to give the body of Christ directions, and even prophetic warnings. They are not self-appointed but recognised by all believers, as having this authority operating quite visibly in their lives! Their prophecies are very weighty and carry an obvious anointing of the Holy Spirit. They also have the ability to declare a thing and see it happen.

Even though they have been released to the greater body of Christ, they will still look for ways to train up others in the global setting whether through conferences, podcasts, books, videos, (and other forms media), while they travel from church to church to minister and bring encouragement and direction. Again – this is NEVER a self-appointed ministry. A person must be recognised – even ordained for this ministry – by the church movement, or group of churches that have recognised this gift to the glory of God and His purposes.

Unfortunately, today we are seeing many well-meaning people who are not recognised prophets, giving their "prophecies" on YouTube and other social media platforms, but who have skipped all the steps and coverings, to become self-proclaimed prophets. Their words are contradictory to recognised prophets and they further add to the confusion to the body of Christ as a whole. Why is this happening? Because there has been little correct teaching on the subject, and little true governance. (Note that Jesus also prophesied that in the last days many false prophets would arise – Matt 24:11,24; Mark 13:22).

You Can't Skip the Process

There are perceivers everywhere. Those who are born perceivers will gravitate to the prophetic quite naturally when they are saved. Those who are not saved will gravitate towards clairvoyancy and other supernatural phenomena. These gifts can be enhanced by the Holy Spirit when saved, or enhanced by the demonic when not. They may merely continue to operate on a low level throughout a person's life, helping them make good personal or business decisions, or just knowing or sensing things are about to happen. Or a person could merely ignore these insights altogether, labelling them as irrational and never paying them much attention.

I had a vision once of walking into this very old train station. Inside there were piles of empty boxes that no one had collected. Then I opened one and this massive ball of bright energy appeared. God was saying that people had been offered many gifts, but so many had either abandoned them from negative or lack of knowledge, misunderstood what they were for, or didn't know they could have them. So, you may have perception but still fail to recognise the gifts the Holt Spirit places within you, and thus, they are never used to the full extend that He intended for you.

Once the gift is stirred up, however, the Holy Spirit can give more until it becomes a passion within. It is then recognised by the church, and may eventually be recognised as fivefold. However, just because you were born a perceiver does not automatically mean you are or even will be a fivefold minister. That's completely up to Jesus and His vision for the church, not you! Besides which, there is always a process that the Holy Spirit takes you through. There may even be sacrifices to be made and testing to ensure you have the character to carry the gift and can be trusted with it. Even so, Jesus said,

> "*Many will say to Me in that day, 'Lord, Lord, have we not prophesied in Your name, cast out demons in Your name, and done many wonders in Your name?' And then I will declare to them, 'I never knew you; depart from Me, you who practice lawlessness!'*" – **Matthew 7:22-23 NKJV**

That being said, there is a caution to be given here. The greatest gift you could desire is not to simply prophesy, but to know God and His love, *to love Him with everything* that you are, and to love others as a result. If you operate in any spiritual gifts without love you and your gift are nothing in God's eyes.

> "*Though I speak with the tongues of men and of angels, but have not love, I have become sounding brass or a clanging cymbal. And though I have the gift of prophecy, and understand all mysteries and all knowledge, and though I have all faith, so that I could remove*

mountains, but have not love, I am nothing." – **1 Corinthians: 1-2 NKJV**

Therefore, the process to being effectively used by God in the "prophetic" (i.e. the vocal and revelation gifts) involves the believer's heart. It should/must be totally focussed on God and not the gift itself, nor your abilities! You are the tool in His hand, for His glory! We partner with Him.

Guidelines, Checks & Balances

So far, this has been a very brief outline of the prophetic and hearing the voice of God. There are always guidelines, and checks & balances to be learned before you take off on your own. Above all, pray for accuracy with no ambiguity in the words He entrusts us to deliver on His behalf. Also, pray for the anointing that His words will achieve the intended purposes of God! There may even be some sacrifices required of you if you are to move on further in your prophetic gift!

One big obstacle to hearing correctly, is the noise you already have absorbed into your brain. We are a generation who have been overdosed on videos, opinions and stories. When we are constantly listening to these things in preference to God's voice, it will be difficult to still those thoughts and hear His. Instead, those will be the thoughts that frame everything else, including how we hear God. I remember a recognised prophet telling me that when the *Chronicles of Narnia* series of books by C. S. Lewis was popularised again via the movies that were released, she also read the books once more. However, at that time, all her prophecies had references and examples from those books. (God uses what you have already in your hand – or in this case, head.)

Note, if you have most of your time given over to other interests and not to God, you will also find it difficult to hear. (See the "*Entanglement*" section of the next chapter "*Hindrances to Faith*".)

If you read and study the word daily, you will begin to recognise the voice of God and whether your prophecy is truly from God. **He will never contradict His word**. It is absolute truth, and there is no reason for Him to lie. Therefore, you can be confident in every word within it. If your prophecy cuts across this, turf it out. It's not from God.

When starting out, you must confirm that it is in fact, the voice of God that you are hearing/seeing/sensing, and not something else. This is why we need one another. They will/should be able to sense God on it or not. In fact, in the early stages of our gift, it is imperative that we are humble enough to **submit our "prophetic" words** to the oversight/leadership/established prophet for scrutiny before launching out on our own. This is for the church's safety.

> "*Without counsel, plans go awry, but in the multitude of counsellors they are established.*" – **Proverbs 15:22 NKJV**

> "*Where there is no counsel, the people fall; But in the multitude of counsellors there is safety.*" – **Proverbs 11:14 NKJV**

(Many churches will post an established prophet at the front of the church for others to approach if they feel God has spoken to them. This is so that they can confirm it is truly the voice of God speaking.) Once we are willing to do this, our gift can be honed,and we will have a feel for what it is like to prophesy with accuracy.

A huge don't for newbies in the prophetic is: **don't** give prophecies containing "***mates, dates, or babes***". In other words, don't give prophecies telling a person who they will marry, nor give specific dates that things will occur, nor whether a person will have a baby, or its gender. So many well-meaning newbies and self-proclaimed prophets have spoken these types of words over people, or congregations, and have ship-wrecked, not just people's faith (since they believe that God honour His promises to them), but lives as a result (disappointments/hope deferred make the heart sick - Proverbs 13:12). Even if you feel strongly about this, be restrained and silent on the matter. You could be wrong!

Also, we should ***avoid giving negative prophecies***. This is because you could get it wrong and destroy a person's character, and cause many other problems. The gifts are there to encourage and build-up of the body, not tear it down. If there's correction, the five-fold prophet or apostle is the one responsible to bring correction, just as Paul did for the Corinthians. If God reveals something negative (e.g. a sin) about another person, He is asking you to intercede on their behalf. This information is generally for you alone, and is not for you to tell everyone, or gather brethren together to pray for that particular person. Again, that is character assassination! If you really feel strongly about something, take it to the leadership, but if there is no physical proof, and they feel God is not on your particular "word" concerning that person, you could be eating humble pie and also discredit your gift. Be very weary of giving any kind of negative words. The enemy loves to use them against us to wreak havoc!! Plus, the words you speak have power. Even being critical in your conversation can have a marked effect, especially if you often see your declarations come to pass.

I once had a reasonably strong prophet say some critical

things about me to another person whilst on a short mission trip to Thailand. (I had challenged them on something previous to this criticism, and they ended up being wrong. Not sure whether this played a part in this or not!) Anyway, I remained silent on the matter of their criticism but felt a real heaviness creep over me, so much so that I prayed from a distance extending my hand, but never actually laying hands on people.

Then one night while the others were out having a meal, I was back in the motel room praying and asking God to reveal to me what was happening. Straight away He said, "*Negative words!*" I hadn't even put two & two together until then, so it was an "*Of course it is!*" revelation. Then I simply prayed and broke off the power of those words and I felt the weight lift, as did my spirits.

Therefore, don't prophesy negatively, PLUS ***refrain from speaking any kind of negativity over people***, either to their face or behind their backs. You are filled with the God who made the entire universe by His Word. As such, the words you speak hold power and weight in the spirit realm. Don't use those words to tear down others but to edify and build them up. Besides, you have not been appointed as a judge by God. Only Jesus has that responsibility!! Not only can your judgements have severe ramifications, but Christ also lives in your brethren, and to criticise them is to criticise Christ!

If you are a seasoned prophet, you may give a "*If you continue to do.... then, but if you do ... then I will...*" type of prophecy that replaces negative with positive. This type of word is totally in line with many prophecies given in the Scriptures, but again for those that have a well-honed gift.

There is always more in the prophetic, but don't try to run

before you can walk. Therefore, avoid giving prophetic words in the carpark, but always ***remain under scrutiny and authority***. Don't get your back up if someone in leadership above you declares they don't believe your prophetic word is from God. Always remain humble and teachable, and if you're right and they're wrong, God will lift you up in due course, for it is His gift to use for His purposes when He wants them used. If someone is blocking those purposes, God will deal with that person, and you won't have to. All you need to do is pray into the situation.

Finally, if someone gives you a personal prophecy, firstly ask yourself who they are. Are they under authority? Are they recognised by their church as a prophet (not necessarily fivefold either), or someone who merely believes they are the mouthpiece of God? How accurate are they known to be? Does this resonate in your spirit as being true. Usually, God will speak directly to you first, and as such, the prophecy is merely a confirmation. (Not always but most of the time!)

Be careful here, as often the very things we have been praying for or desiring, can be like strong thoughts in our spirits, that others might "hear" in the spirit, and subsequently, jump to conclusions that this is a "prophesy" from God, when in fact, it's not. They perceived it, but it was not prophetic. Many people have been walked down the proverbial "garden path" by this kind of prophecy, and ended up in bitter disappointment when their requests have not manifested.

If the one giving the "prophecy" is not a seasoned prophet, remember that the enemy can speak in the spirit too, and may give you a false prophecy. (This is why it is important for you to also know how to hear from God for yourself.) Therefore, unless you absolutely trust this prophet for their accuracy and integrity, don't hold tightly to their prophecy. Rather, take it before the Lord. Obviously, if it doesn't feel right in your spirit (especially if it is negative), be willing to release it or even reject it. Otherwise, put it on the back-burner until God confirms or denies it in other ways.

To know even more on this topic, I strongly suggest further reading and teaching on all aspects of hearing God's voice so that you can be well grounded and confident in the delivery and right handling of the messages from God, and are also able to discern whether the words other people speak over you are legitimate or not.

Remember, this is not a gift for your own personal use but to use in ***partnership with the Holy Spirit and for His Glory alone!*** It is a tool for the kingdom and will pass away. What matters most is your personal motivation when using the gifts (1 Corinthians 13:2), and that your heart is right before God!

Regardless of all this, rather than to wander too far off topic at this point, I have only included this teaching to help you understand how to hear accurately. (I strongly suggest further reading and teaching on all aspects of hearing God's voice so that you can be well grounded and confident in the delivery and right handling of messages from God.)

In relation to faith, it is my hope that this teaching will enable you to stand unshakably on the words and promises that God gives you personally, knowing that He is faithful, reliable and totally truthful. If you are constantly disappointed, you are either incorrectly basing your faith on a false premise, have misunderstood what God was trying to tell you, or have not heard God at all. Better to get it right first time around.

Chapter 3

Hinderances to Faith

~~~~~~~~~~~~~~

Hinderance to faith come in all shapes and sizes. Some are disappointments, some are misplaced expectations, even fear and worry play a big part, but wilful disobedience and sin can destroy our faith as it puts our attention on us and our needs and not squarely on God. Needless to say, in this chapter I want to address some reasons why we do not receive the things we are hoping for, or the answers to our prayer. Some are hinderances, other blockages and others still, are faith destroying.

Fear & Worry

God has not given us a spirit of fear (2 Timothy 1:7). In fact, His perfect love casts out all fear (1 John 4:18). Fear is a tool of the enemy to take your eyes off God and focus on the problem. The enemy wants to destroy tour faith. Remember that Hebrews states

> "*But without faith it is impossible to please Him, for he who comes to God must believe that He is, and that He is a rewarder of those who diligently seek Him.*" – **Hebrews 11:6 NKJV**

Why do we fear when we know that our God can do anything, even the impossible? Well, sometimes we just see the problem as too large. It could be that people are constantly pressuring us and causing us great emotional stress. It may be our finances are too low to cover the bills. It may be something we desperately need but the time is already at
~~~~~~~~~~~~~~

the 11th hour and we can't see how possibly this can work out for good. There are many worries in this life, but the one sure anchor is our God.

When our eyes can only see the problem, we become double minded. We know in our heads that God is able to do exceedingly abundantly above all we ask or think (Ephesians 3:20), but in our hearts we are still worried about the negative outcome. This speaks of a lack of trust in God and who He is.

> "*But let him ask in faith, with no doubting, for he who doubts is like a wave of the sea driven and tossed by the wind. For let not that man suppose that he will receive anything from the Lord; he is a double-minded man, unstable in all his ways.*" - **James 1:6-8 NKJV**

Double mindedness, will not produce a good outcome, and the enemy loves to feed our fear and worry because he knows this. So how do we deal with this? How can we stop the fears?

As mentioned, perfect love casts out all fear. That is, when we draw closer to God, we begin to see who He really is and know in our heart of hearts how He will respond to our requests. Another fear eradicator is to listen to testimonies. God did it for others, He can do it for you. Yet another is to praise God constantly in order to place your attention squarely upon Him. Reading His word and allowing the Holy Spirit to encourage you through it, will also help to build up your faith. Finally, reciting aloud Scriptures that proclaim His promises as a reminder to yourself of His goodness, will also build up your faith. Paul states,

> "*So, then faith comes by hearing, and hearing by the word of God.*" – **Romans 10:17 - NKJV**

These are all fear busters, that put your eyes back on God and away from your problem. They will give you that quiet assurance that you know that you know. When fear tries to regain a foothold, you can tell the enemy that he is a liar and that your God is a good and truthful God, and will see His words and promises fulfilled.

Disappointments

Disappointments happen because our expectations are not fulfilled, or in this case, we may have had situations where our "faith" has proven fruitless, and now wonder why it didn't work for us. After repeated attempts and disappointments, we become discouraged. The Bible even says that,

> "*Hope deferred makes the heart sick, but when the desire comes, it is a tree of life.*" – Proverbs 13:12 NKJV

Another way of saying this, is that repeated disappointments can become discouraging to our faith in God.

What if you did have faith and nothing happened? Sometimes, we've not asked according to His will and asked amiss.

> "*Now this is the confidence that we have in Him, that if we ask anything according to His will, He hears us. And if we know that He hears us, whatever we ask, we know that we have the petitions that we have asked of Him.*" – **1 John 5:14-15 NKJV**

> "*You ask and do not receive, because you ask amiss, that you may spend it on your pleasures.*" – **James 4:3 NKJV**

At other times we are not willing to believe that God has said, "No!" This is one of the reasons why we should persist in prayer. We need to hear just what God is saying about our request, otherwise we are not walking in faith but presumption. How many things have fallen in a heap because we presumed the answer was "Yes!", but God had not given us that answer, our own desires did!

After we are sure, we should accept the outcome and thank Him despite what the answer is. Who knows, His "No!" may have just saved you unnecessary pain and destruction to your faith. This "No" was given out of God's goodness and love for you! Therefore, giving thanks in either situation is very important.

> "*Rejoice always, pray without ceasing, in everything give thanks; for this is the will of God in Christ Jesus for you.*" – **1 Thessalonians 5:16-18 NKJV**

Timing

I need to also add here, that disappointments can occur because our timing may not be God's timing. As humans, as soon as we catch the ball, we want to run with it. Instead of waiting to hear God add the, "*...but not yet*" to His answer. We simply assume any "Yes" He's given us is for now. Then we get upset and disappointed because we don't see it manifest straight away. We seldom sit down and ask God,

> "*Did you mean 'Yes' for now or later? If I do have to wait, how long can I expect this wait to be? Is the length of the wait, determined by me – where I'm at, what I do, - or perhaps even by other people? Is there anything I need to do to prepare for this, first? How can I partner with Your will, Lord?*"

The last couple of questions are especially relevant if you know that God has called you to the ministry, or to the mission field. There are obvious things you need to do to prepare. Perhaps attending Bible College, or applying for a passport, and so on.

Overall, disappointments are most often our own fault because we have asked amiss (not in line with His will) or didn't realise that there would be a wait for the answer in God's timing. However, the wait can also be because of delays created by the enemy to make us believe that God will not do as He promised, or that we are not of any value to Him that He should bother to give us that for which we asked.

The Delays

However, more often than not, there are delays which suggest we need to persist in prayer and not cave into any disappointment or negative thoughts about God's promises. As mentioned, the devil wants you to doubt God's goodness and love towards you, and God's good character. He'll try everything to make you give up, and to make you lose faith. You can't afford to listen. You must continue to persist and have faith, no matter how long it takes. If God has said it, we must believe Him – just like Abraham did, even if the circumstances in the natural appear to be contrary to a favourable outcome.

For example: During CoVid, the price of housing rose suddenly and steeply. This meant that many people with investment housing that were tenanted, chose to sell their properties in order to pay off their loans and in so doing, also make a profit from the inflated selling prices.

The flow on effect here in Australia was to cause a shortage of available rental houses on the market. Not only that, but for the houses still being tenanted, most landlords took advantage of the shortages and the extreme hike in market prices, to raise rental costs by huge increments. This, in turn, forced many tenants out of homes, causing the demand for new accommodations to rise even more significantly in what had become a very shrunken rental market.

(There were other factors that caused the housing shortage as well. Many lost their jobs because of vaccine mandates and had to break their current leases to find other cheaper housing. In Queensland, as soon as the borders we reopened, we also had an influx of people migrating from other states that had had extreme lockdown measures in place. Because the price escalation began at the start of the year, the market demand was higher due to university students seeking accommodations before the academic year commenced, and those families that were moving during school holidays for whatever reason, were also on the hunt for housing as well.)

Unfortunately, our landlord also wanted to raise our rent over $230 per week at the end of our current lease. My husband works full-time, which meant it was left to me to find something cheaper. Although I had been to inspect several rental houses, and filled out copious applications, our applications were not even making it to the top of the assessment pile before the house was leased to other people.

Myself and even others had prayed many prayers into this, and believed God would not leave us stranded, but as the vacate deadline quickly approached, it became more and more apparent in the natural sphere, that we would have nowhere else to go. The reality of the situation is that there were already many displaced people living in tents on the beach because not only were rental properties in short supply, but even alternative accommodation like motels, or caravan/camping parks and so on, were completely full and simply unavailable. "*There's no room at the inn. Sorry! Move along!*" This was the same situation Mary and Joseph were faced with. However, we all know that out of the seemingly hopeless situation they faced, being forced to sleep in a stable, God presented His most precious Son to the world – a miracle above all we could hope for.

Our exit deadline was set to a Tuesday in June and it was now the Friday just prior to it. It normally takes a couple of weeks from the processing of applications, to obtaining the keys and shifting in. The agent waits until they have all the applications. (However, if there are numerous applications to check, they might only look at the first few, which I suspect was the case for the most part.) After the applications are sorted, what the agent considers to be the best prospects, are shortlisted and these applications (after references and details are checked) are sent through to the owner to peruse and pick who they consider to be the best applicant. The owner then contacts the agent to continue negotiations with the chosen applicant, who is notified in writing.

At this time, the prospective tenant must pay the bond (which is equivalent to 4 weeks rent) plus 2 weeks rent in advance. Then and only then, when the money is paid, can the final stages commence. This includes the agent walking through the property while recording any previous damage, and imperfections in the property. A lease is then drawn up and handed with the agent's entry report for the tenant to sign, and finally, the keys handed over. The usual time for this process is generally around two weeks.

Unfortunately for us, at this juncture, we only had 4 days

to be shifted out and completely moved into the new place. (This includes time to thoroughly clean the house to Residential Tenancy Association (RTA) standards after the house is vacated.) It looked impossible. However, I wasn't panicking. I felt as if God had us in His hand, because He is a good Father.

On that Friday morning, for some reason I looked again at the rental ads. There was a newly listed house that might suit our needs, but they were not even offering viewings until the Tuesday, by which time we needed to be out of our current rental. Nevertheless, I rang the real estate agent on the off chance that we might be able to view it earlier than Tuesday. I explained the situation to her and she told me that she would discuss it with the owner and call me back. In the meantime, I sent through an application and our particulars. The following day we viewed the property, we were approved, bond moneys were paid and we collected the keys on the Monday afternoon. It was a miracle. It never happens that quickly!

I could have given up, but I believed in God's goodness. I could do nothing else. Did I have faith in *my* prayer request? No, I simply had faith in God's goodness despite what the situation looked like. However, that faith was tested until well passed the eleventh hour - to a time that was no longer humanly possible.

Lack of Persistence

I've actually heard a person say,

> *"If I've asked God for something once, isn't it a lack of faith to ask a second time?"*

That sounds logical except for the fact that Jesus told us to be persistent. (See how man's wisdom sometimes opposes God's) Why? Because there is an enemy who can block prayers and outcomes. Sometimes there's an unseen battle going on, and our prayers are part of the battle. The more we trust God for the outcome, even though it's being held up, the more likely the outcome will be positive.

Remember Daniel who prayed for 3 weeks.

> "*In those days I, Daniel, was mourning three full weeks. I ate no pleasant food, no meat or wine came into my mouth, nor did I anoint myself at all, till three whole weeks were fulfilled...*
>
> [12]*Then he said to me, 'Do not fear, Daniel, for from the first day that you set your heart to understand, and to humble yourself before your God, your words were heard; and I have come because of your words. But the prince of the kingdom of Persia withstood me twenty-one days; and behold, Michael, one of the chief princes, came to help me, for I had been left alone there with the kings of Persia.*'" – **Daniel 10:2-3, 12-13 NKJV**

The angel told him that God had given His answer the day Daniel asked, but the devil was delaying the outcome. Did Daniel stop praying after the first day? No! He kept at it until His prayer was answered.

Now since that happened to Daniel, it can happen to us too. It can be a battle – literally – in the spirit realm, and we need to keep praying for the outcome. If we give up before we see the manifestation of our requests, we can empower the enemy by our negativity, and lose both the battle and the answer to our request. The devil will always try to stop the answer, or twist our thinking enough for us to abandon hope if he can.

Do I have a Scripture verse to back up that statement? Yes! Remember Zacharias when he was visited by the angel Gabrielle who told him that he and his wife would have a child, (John the Baptist)? When Zacharias became negative and started to object because of their old age, the angel made him mute. John's miraculous birth was part of God's perfect plan and no verbal/spoken negativity would be allowed to prevent things running their course.

Likewise, our negativity empowers the evil one to stop the answer to prayer. He's a master of deception. We often believe the enemy's deceptive delays over and above the goodness of God. We, in essence, will unconsciously imply (or even say directly) that God's word isn't true, or He doesn't love us because we are somehow sub-optimal and/or faulty merchandise, or worse, that Jesus didn't die for us, or God made a mistake when He chose us. Can you see how this is anti-faith, and slaps God in the face? Not only is this totally refutable in God's Word, but it displays a lack of understanding of God's character, and your own identity in Christ. Remember the Word says that it is no longer you who live but Christ who lives in you.

> "*I have been crucified with Christ; it is no longer I who live, but Christ lives in me; and the life which I now live in the flesh I live by faith in the Son of God, who loved me and gave Himself for me.*" - **Galatians 2:20 NKJV**

If you now denigrate yourself, aren't you also denigrating Christ in you?

We must sometimes be like the persistent widow who keeps at it, and not be too quick to give up. At the end of the parable of the persistent widow in Luke 18:1-8, Jesus questioned whether He, upon His return, He would find this kind of *faith* on earth. Why? Because this generation is the "*now*" generation more than ever before. We have everything at the click of a button. Patience is no longer a virtue to be prized. Nevertheless, Jesus has asked us to *persist* – to knock and keep knocking, to call forth those things that are unseen as though they were, and to trust in Him (in His promises, whether in His Word of that you've received in prayer), and to trust His goodness and generosity towards those He loves.

Now I Have It, Now I Don't

There are times when a person is healed and a day or two later experiences those same symptoms back again. God is not an "Indian Giver". Those symptoms are a lie, tailored to convince you to accept the illness back. As soon as you agree, you've handed the invitation to the infirmity to make it true, and it greedily accepts and barges his way back in the door.

I remember being told of a young woman (I knew this woman and the preacher involved) who had had constant kidney problems, and who was subsequently prayed for during a church meeting. She was miraculously healed, but a couple of days later she puffed up like a balloon again, and all the symptoms returned. Thankfully she was at church again when it took place. The church again prayed for her, only this time nothing happened. That was odd! Why was the infirmity back, and now, why wouldn't it leave? They'd prayed in the same manner as the first time that had seen a great healing take place. They were also confident that they would see the same result this time, and yet nothing.

Given the seriousness of the woman's seemingly worsening condition, they were about to set out for the hospital when the pastor, inspired by the Holy Spirit, spun around pointing at the young woman and cried out angrily, "*This is a lie!*" Immediately, the swelling disappeared and her kidneys were back to normal. The infirmity wasn't really back. The evidence was false! No wonder all their prayers were fruitless. She was already healed. The evil spirit behind this was just deceiving the person into speaking out the health condition in order for the infirmity to re-gain its foothold.

The keys to avoiding possible disappointments, are to keep praying until we get an answer, but also to also thank God continually for the manifestation of the answer after you've *received confirmation* that it's God's good pleasure to give you what you've asked for. Then, even if the enemy wants to convince you that you don't really have the answer (even after it has already manifested, as in the case of the healing above), you just tell him he's a liar, and to keep thanking God for the answer. In the end, it's all about trust in God. Also remember that what comes out of your mouth can determine the ultimate outcome of your prayer requests.

Disobedience

We all slip up from time to time and make mistakes, but that is not to what I'm referring. When these things occur, and we realise what we've done, most Christians will be quick to ask for forgiveness and deal with this kind of sin mistake. However, constant wilfulness and disobedience are another matter. These will cause our hearts to harden to the prompting of the Holy Spirit. The more often this occurs the harder our hearts become. As Christians we all know this. However, what is less obvious is the inverse link between faith and hardness of heart. David warns us of this:

> *"Do not harden your hearts, as in the rebellion, as in the day of trial in the wilderness."* – **Psalm 95:7b-8 - NKJV**

The hardening of hearts and rebelliousness are very much linked. Hebrews 3 describes how the Israelites tested and tried God, for their hearts were hard and full of unbelief (i.e. lack of faith.) They instead complained that God had brought them into the desert to kill them. Even though God had demonstrated His power and that He would keep His covenant with Abraham (i.e. He was totally reliable), because they didn't really know Him, they had no faith, only fear and superstition. Faith is based on who God is and His demonstrated favour towards us, but what the Israelites were demonstrating was anti-faith in action, which produced even more hardness of heart.

If we cannot fathom the things of God via our human reasoning, it is easy to become skeptical and fall into unbelief, just like the Israelites, hardening our hearts to the truth and to the Giver of truth. (In a sense this is elevating our own opinions and thoughts above God's, which is pride at best.) Even telling yourself that God probably won't heal you, is not just telling God He is a liar, but unbelief grows stronger when our lack of faith produces a lack of positive outcomes (i.e. no answers to prayers). This constant disappointment hardens the heart for the next time we need an answer, and continues to do so until our hearts are very hard and sick, and faith abandoned.

> *"Hope deferred makes the heart sick, but when the desire comes, it is a tree of life."* – **Proverbs 13:12 NKJV**

The hardening of our hearts can also originate from worldly ideas, or even worldly wants and desires. Are we allowing the world to develop our minds and thinking, and are hearts desires, or are we renewing our minds via the Word of God? Paul tells us to think about good things not bad.

> "*Finally, brethren, whatever things are true, whatever things are noble, whatever things are just, whatever things are pure, whatever things are lovely, whatever things are of good report, if there is any virtue and if there is anything praiseworthy—meditate on these things.*" - **Philippians 4:8 NKJV**

Conversely, to think on worldly things will lead to sin. This is why we are told to renew our minds in the word of God.

> "*And do not be conformed to this world, but be transformed by the renewing of your mind, that you may prove what is that good and acceptable and perfect will of God.*" - **Romans 12:2 NKJV**

Further, when we encourage one another in the Word of God, we are also countering/negating any worldly ideas with the truth of Christ Jesus. Not only does this encourage us in our walk and strengthens our faith, but prevents our hearts from hardening.

The tell-tale signs or manifestations of a hardened heart are willful sin and disobedience. Allowed to continue unchecked, a hardening heart can cause in a complete loss of faith as the person turns away from God and begins justifying their sin.

You might consider it completely incongruous for a Christian who loves God and has served Him for some time, to even begin to think of carrying out something they know is completely wrong before God, but it often begins with the smallest step across the line. A little compromise here, and a little compromise there. We tell ourselves that it is not that bad: "*only a little white lie*", and "*only the one time and small amount, cheating on my tax*", "*I never actually said something untruthful – simply implied it*", and "*it's only an admiring glance at that good looking person who is not my spouse*". No harm done right? Wrong!

The very next time we are faced with a similar situation, we've already convinced ourselves that it wasn't so bad last time, and hey, we got away with it! Thus, we have no qualms about repeating the offence. In this way we are searing our conscience with a hot iron (see 1Timothy 4:2) and hardening our hearts to the truth by our constant self-justification.

Before long we will be doing those things we always considered totally wrong for Christians to be doing. Ask anyone who has fallen into the trap of having an affair. It didn't start out intentionally, but with a small step across the line of what was acceptable behaviour and what was totally inappropriate! Could be as simple as just going out for lunch with a fellow employee of the opposite sex. Then another and another lunch, then after work drinks and then dinner, then meeting up for other events and activities, and so on. Before you realise it, you're in over your head, and you don't want to stop. It has become willful sin.

Obviously, if we deliberately choose sin over God's will for us, it indicates a much deeper heart issue, since, as noted earlier, when we truly love God, we have no desire to do anything that would disappoint Him.

> "*He who has My commandments and keeps them, it is*

he who loves Me." – **John 14:21a NKJV**

Nevertheless, the more we choose the world and its ways, the more distant we become to God in our hearts, and faith in Him is over written by self-reliance. As also noted earlier, the more we desire the world, the less hungry we are for God, BUT the more we put God first in our lives, the more we hunger and thirst after Him. The more we seek God and begin to know Him more, the more faith we will have in Him. Conversely, the more we sin and desire to sin, the harder our hearts become, and our consciences becomes seared, with unbelief following close behind.

Therefore, our faith is destroyed the more our hearts are hardened whether it begins with disappointments or manifests in willful disobedience.

However, Paul states that if we walk in the Spirit we will not fulfill the lusts of the flesh.

> "*I say then: Walk in the Spirit, and you shall not fulfill the lust of the flesh.*" - **Galatians 5:16 NKJV**

Listen to what the psalmist says,

> "*Your word I have hidden in my heart, That I might not sin against You.*" – **Psalm 119:11 - NKJV**

What is it to hide the Scriptures in our heart? The memorisation of Scripture, though not as popular as it once was, is extremely useful, or pushing passed the temptations to sin. Even Jesus countered with "*It is written...*" when tempted by the devil in the wilderness.

The Scriptures are powerful. Only with the constant washing of the Word, can we remain in His will and maintain our faith in Him.

> "*Then Jesus said to those Jews who believed Him, 'If you abide in My word, you are My disciples indeed. And you shall know the truth, and the truth shall make you free.'*" – **John 8:31-32 NKJV**

To abide, means to live there. In context, abiding in His word is to read it often, thinking and meditating upon it as we do, and to encourage each other in it, especially if we receive a rhema revelation from it. It also means that if we do not understand, even after considerable time cogitating over and cross referencing the Scripture, we ask/pray the Holy Spirit to enlighten us concerning its meaning. (Should do that from the start actually.) Then after having done all this, we should apply and do those things that the Word has stated and/or the Holy Spirit has revealed to us. This application of His Word reinforces the Word in us, and seeing the positive outcomes that result, gives us the impetus to keep reading it and renewing our thinking in it. Psalm 119 says:

> "*Oh, how I love Your law! It is my meditation all the day. You, through Your commandments, make me wiser than my enemies; for they are ever with me. I have more understanding than all my teachers, for Your testimonies are my meditation. I understand more than the ancients, because I keep Your precepts.*" – **Psalm 119:97-100 NKJV**

To abide in His Word keeps our hearts soft and our actions pure. When our hearts are soft before God, we recognise His love for us, and love Him more in return, which flows over in acts of service to others and obedience to Him.

I want to also point out that as we await the last great outpouring, we need to consider the ramifications of disobedience and subsequent lack of faith in God. The Holy Spirit is grieved by sin. Therefore, we cannot pray for revival, even with expectancy and some semblance of faith, and still continue in disobedience and willful sin. It's like asking the Holy Spirit to rest in a filthy temple. It's totally dishonouring and it grieves Him.

Imagine with me that a brother or sister in Christ whom you dearly love, has asked you over for coffee one night to discuss some things. You haven't seen them for some time as they attend a different church and now live about an hour away across town. So naturally you are eager to accept the invitation. You also have never been to their new house, so are also keen to see how they are doing.

When your host opens the door, you notice a strong musty smell, but pay little attention. However, as you walk inside, you begin to notice that the place is absolutely filthy. You are led to the kitchen-dining-family area and take a seat at the dining table. From there you can see that there are dishes not just in the sink but piled on the bench. The garbage bin is over flowing and stinks to high heavens. Everywhere you look you see dust, dirt and mess. Nevertheless, because you love this person, you sit down at the table with them to talk.

Your host/hostess later rises from the table to fill the kettle, and puts it on to boil. However, they discover there are no clean cups. Not to worry, you offer to wash up, but the host/hostess, tells you not to bother and that they'd simply rinse off two cups instead. When the beverage is ready for the milk, they open the fridge, and the worst smells wafts out. You notice that there are foodstuffs there that should have been thrown out long ago, but your host/hostess smells the carton of milk and deeming it to still be ok, finishes making the coffee.

All good (you hope). You have a wonderful conversation and communion with your friend, but it's now getting very late and you really need to head home. However, the host/hostess then has a brilliant idea: they ask you to stay the night. Before you've had a chance to respond, they are showing you the spare room right down the back of the house. It not only smells very musty, but the bed linen looks like it's never been washed. What's worse is that there is mould on the roof and there's a cat litter tray in the corner, that really needs emptying.

However, the host/hostess doesn't think twice about the condition of the room. They're more excited that you might stay. Although you love them dearly, how would you respond? I doubt that you would feel like accepting the invitation. Some even might feel disrespected that they should be asked to sleep in the dirtiest and most forgotten/neglected room in the house.

I'm sure you can see where I'm going with this. Often, we expect the Holy Spirit to be happy to stay in our temple, even though it may have been neglected and filled with all kind of worldly stuff that grieves Him.

How did it get to that state? A little here and a little there, somethings never dealt with that should have been and were perhaps even ignored!

Perhaps there are hurts that have never really been dealt with (we prefer not to think about it) but those hurts are full of unforgiveness (I will deal separately with this topic at the end of this chapter) that can breed bitterness without you realising it.

Perhaps there's regret because *you* never took the time to ask for forgiveness from someone else. You'd simply hoped that time would fix the relationship. It was just too uncomfortable knowing the hurt you caused, to even broach the subject again, and now the distance between you has grown even greater.

Perhaps there are habits that you never thought were that bad and didn't require any work, or cleaning up. However, now these habits are leading to other kinds of negative behaviours. However, because we are so used to them, we just see them as normal.

When we park ourselves in front of the TV or YouTube or other tech, we are letting the world enter our own home. Perverse ideas are filling our heads and changing our thinking without us realising it. These things are like dirty dishes that are slowly growing mouldy. Little foxes destroying the vine. They largely go unnoticed but damage is being done. The entertainment industry is becoming so perverse now, we need to be very careful what we watch and listen to. The dishes have been piling up on the bench and beginning to stink. In Psalms it says,

> "*I will lead a life of integrity in my own home. I will refuse to look at anything vile and vulgar. I hate all who deal crookedly; I will have nothing to do with them. I will reject perverse ideas and stay away from every evil.*" - **Psalm 101:2-4 NLT**

The Holy Spirit keeps suggesting that He will help to wash the dishes and fix the issues, but we think we're fine and maybe we'll fix it later. It's too much effort at the moment. We can always clean a cup here or a dish there when needed but nothing that requires sacrifice and personal cost.

All of these things grieve the Holy Spirit, and worse are indicative of the state of our heart, how much we love God, how much we prioritise Him, and how much we seek to honour Him.

Besides all that, sin has consequences, and not just a lowering of our faith. I want you to consider with me, the story of Ananias and Saphira. It may seem a little off the topic of faith, but it is connected. God hates sin and disobedience. If we sin wilfully, that is knowing full well that what we are doing is wrong or against God's will, we are in fact spitting in God's face. When we love Him, we will be willing to do whatever He wants, knowing that His yoke is easy and His burden is light.

> "*Take My yoke upon you and learn from Me, for I am gentle and lowly in heart, and you will find rest for your souls. For My yoke is easy and My burden is light.*" – **Matthew 11:29,30 NKJV**

However, when we choose to sin, it speaks volumes about our love for Him, and how we view God, and even how we view ourselves in His sight. For example: If we *believe* God *won't* give us anything, and therefore, we need to do something wrong (e.g. lie, cheat, steal etc.) for personal gain, it shows a big lack of faith right there. Remember that God is able to do exceedingly abundantly above all we say or think (Ephesians 3:20). Also, He has provided us with all we need. Therefore, we have no need to sin.

> "*His divine power has given to us all things that pertain to life and godliness, through the knowledge of Him who called us by glory and virtue.*" – **2 Peter 1:3 NKJV**

Faith and sin are inversely proportional. The more you sin,

the less inclined to have faith in God you will be. The more your faith is built up, the less you'll want to sin, because your faith is based on your intimate knowledge of God. Therefore, to discuss sin, is not really off topic.

Now before I go any further, and start to discuss Annanias and Saphirra, I don't wish to guilt-trip anyone. My place is not to point the finger, and be judgemental or condemning. God is the only judge. I merely wish to make a rather sobering point for you to consider.

Let's look at this portion of Scripture to ascertain what exactly is going on here and what are out take aways from it.

> "*But a certain man named Ananias, with Sapphira his wife, sold a possession. And he kept back part of the proceeds, his wife also being aware of it, and brought a certain part and laid it at the apostles' feet.*
>
> *But Peter said, "Ananias, why has Satan filled your heart to lie to the Holy Spirit and keep back part of the price of the land for yourself? While it remained, was it not your own? And after it was sold, was it not in your own control? Why have you conceived this thing in your heart? You have not lied to men but to God."*
>
> *Then Ananias, hearing these words, fell down and breathed his last. So great fear came upon all those who heard these things. And the young men arose and wrapped him up, carried him out, and buried him.*
>
> *Now it was about three hours later when his wife came in, not knowing what had happened. And Peter answered her, "Tell me whether you sold the land for so much?" She said, "Yes, for so much." Then Peter said to her, "How is it that you have agreed together to test the Spirit of the Lord? Look, the feet of those who have*

buried your husband are at the door, and they will carry you out."

Then immediately she fell down at his feet and breathed her last. And the young men came in and found her dead, and carrying her out, buried her by her husband. So great fear came upon all the church and upon all who heard these things.

And through the hands of the apostles many signs and wonders were done among the people. And they were all with one accord in Solomon's Porch. Yet none of the rest dared join them, but the people esteemed them highly. And believers were increasingly added to the Lord, multitudes of both men and women." – **Acts 5:1-14 NKJV**

Upon reading this passage, no doubt you've probably thought, "*Wow! That's a pretty heavy punishment for such a seemingly small thing! It's not as if it was rape, or murder or some other equally evil crime!*" My thoughts initially too! Even so, I use to find this passage particularly unsettling and tried to avoid it as much as possible.

However, one day as I was studying the book of Acts, instead of skipping that part, I asked the Holy Spirit what was really going on and about why the punishment was so harsh. His answer may astonish you.

Around the time of the incident, the Christian church (known as the "Way" or the sect of the Nazarene) was in its fledgling years. Although a few thousand souls were added at Pentecost etc, from a global perspective (which was Jesus' vision for His church – that all men might come to know the Father), it was still very small and localised in Jerusalem.

We read just prior to this incident in chapter 4, that the church shared all things I common. In fact, Barnabas, a disciple and pillar of character and reputation, sold all he had and laid the proceeds at the feet of the apostles, to be used for the work of the Kingdom and in the daily distribution. Indeed, this distribution assisted many of the poor who came to Christ.

At this point, we must also remember that Israel suffered under the lash of the Roman whip. They were a subjugated people and taxed heavily by Rome, which was hungrily devouring finances to cover its war machine in the expansion of its Empirical territories. It was the conquered peoples who meet that cost. Subsequently, poverty was common place.

Consequently, for the onlookers/unchurched, being a Christian was a means of being taken care of. The Christians even had a daily distribution, free meals and many

Early Church	**End Times Church**
Fledgling Church	GlobalChurch
First outpouring: - Holy Spirit was essential in building the church	Last outpouring: - More urgent *need* for a greater infilling in the dark end times
God wanted their attention because: * Sin is not acceptable for continuation of Church * Church growth must be protected	God still wants our attention because: * Sin makes us deaf to Holy Spirit's leading * We may miss out when He returns

other of their needs met. What a winning ticket for those who were struggling financially! Just become a Christian and life becomes so much more improved!

It's easy to imagine that there were many "hangers on" as a result – people who had not totally committed to Jesus but were there for selfish reasons. You only need to read John chapter 6 about those who followed Jesus to the other side of the lake after Jesus had fed the five thousand. He was quick to point out that they were only looking for Him merely because they had their bellies filled and were now looking for more. (John 6:26) Again, hangers on looking for what they could get!

Now consider Ananias and Saphirra. Why would they want to be seen as giving to the cause, but not willing to give everything. They obviously weren't there for a free lunch, since they were willing to furnish the church with some of the money from the sale of their house. Were they hoping to gain the same notoriety and respect as Barnabas had, and possibly be seen as some kind of spiritual leaders? Who knows for sure, but it is obvious that something was wrong with their motive and their heart. (Remember what Peter said to Ananias, "*Ananias, why has* ***Satan filled your heart*** *to lie to the Holy Spirit?*")

We do know that they were under no compulsion to give. Peter even tells them, that before the sale, their property was theirs, and even after the sale, the money was still theirs to do whatever they chose to do with it. But instead of telling it like it was, they lied, not just to Peter, but to the Holy Spirit, which ended in their deaths.

This incident put great fear in all those contemplating joining the cause for their own free lunch, the hangers on who were not there because they loved God, but for what they could get, (verse 13). Nevertheless, there were still the genuine converts, who were willing to give even their lives in order to have Christ, and their numbers continued to grow, (verse 14).

Was this a necessary example to make, given the extreme nature of the punishment? Yes! First of all, God is just! Paul tells us that a little leaven spoils the lump, (1 Corinthians 5:6). Because the church was still small and only in the one location, (i.e. they all met together in one place), to leave such sin/leaven within the church, would ultimately cause the entire church's corruption and final destruction from within. Thus, the church would have not survived for very long at all. All that Christ died to achieve would have been obliterated by sin. As painful and hard as it seemed at the time, God had to surgically remove the infection in order to protect the church – the work of His Son.

To further this point, after the incident, although the onlookers highly respected the apostles and the work they did, those unwilling to change and give their hearts genuinely over to Christ, were too afraid to become part of the group, lest their own hearts were exposed and something bad happened to them too. The "hangers on" problem was solved. Now the converts were only those who didn't care whether it cost them their lives, they just wanted Jesus and were willing to give Him their all. (We still see this kind of devotion today in countries where Christians are persecuted and more often than not, killed. Unfortunately, it is mostly in the western nations that Christians have a more lacks approach to sin.)

Not long after the Ananias & Saphirra incident, the church came under intense persecution and there were those who did lose their lives. However, this persecution also caused many good men to disperse and spread the gospel message to those in other towns and cities, and even to other countries. Those churches still had issues that the disciples needed to address, yes, but now the problems were local and did not affect the church as a whole. God had destroyed the root before it could destroy the church. It was a kind of cleansing or purifying of the church to ensure it continued.

Okay, that was two thousand years ago. What does that have to do with us today? Are there any lessons we can take away from this account?

That was at the start of the church age, and we are on the precipice of the close of the church age. The early church commenced with the first outpouring of the Holy Spirit. Now, at the end, many look forward to a last great outpouring of the Holy Spirit, or at least a greater infilling to help us navigate the darkness of these end-times.

At the beginning of the church age, the church was a small fledgling church and needing to grow with the power of the Holy Spirit working through them. Now at the end of the age, the church is a global phenomenon, awaiting the Bridegroom to take us to His home, but because the world has become totally corrupt, we still need the Holy Spirit to give us wisdom for these times, and to also help make us ready while there is still time before He returns. (Eph 5:26-27; 1 Tim 6:13-14; Rev 19:7)

In the early church God was trying to get their attention – giving them a wake-up call to holiness so that He could protect His church. Although we may not see another incident like Annanias & Sapphira, God is still trying to get our attention. Why? Because we are running out of time.

We all know that there are grave consequences for willful-

ness and disobedience, but I believe these consequences will become more and more serious as the Holy Spirit urgently tries to wake us up to purity before the church age swiftly approaches its end.
How can I possibly make such a bold statement? We can get used to the little slaps on the wrist for minor infractions to the point that we now ignore them. But there's so little time to straighten up our act.

Think of a parent who has been constantly trying to make their child do the right thing. Eventually, the punishment will be far more severe in order for that child to come to their senses and realise the harsh consequences of their willfulness. It may just start with a warning. The next time it may be a gentle slap on the wrist and a rebuke. The following time it may mean being sent to its room, then after that, certain privileges may be revoked.

Likewise, God wants us ready. We may have been ignoring His chastising, but He is not willing that we should perish. Allowing a more severe punishment may be the only loving course of action left to wake us up and put us on the right track before it's too late. Only the miracle working power of the God – the cleansing blood of Christ's cross, and changing our hearts by the Holy Spirit through the Word of God and prayer, can possibly save us.

Some will say, "*We've been saved and washed in the blood of the Lamb. We are already clean.*" But I would ask you to remember the passage of Scripture in John 13:4-17, when Jesus washed the disciples' feet.

Peter initially wouldn't allow Jesus to wash his feet, but Jesus replied that what He was doing they did not understand at the time, but they would later. Peter protested even more so, but Jesus answered him "*If I do not wash you,*

you have no part with Me!"

Then Peter, startled by this response, declared that since that was the case, Jesus should wash his head and hands as well. What did Jesus answer?

> *"He who is bathed needs only to wash his feet, but is completely clean; and you are clean, but not all of you."*

This has nothing to do with physical bathing but Spiritual cleansing. (Jesus didn't come to give lessons in hygiene but to teach them about His Father.) Peter was already clean because of the washing of the Word and time spent with Jesus. Therefore, he only needed his "feet" washed. But what does having your feet washed have to do about anything? Is there a deeper meaning? What does it mean spiritually to have your feet washed?

We have been washed at salvation, but we get dirty "feet" as we walk around in the world. Sometimes we walk in mud and are really messed up. Sometimes that mud is so thick and sticky, it's hard to get out of that worldly situation and we need the Holy Spirit to throw us a lifeline before we sink completely. We need our feet washed clean, and our entanglement removed. If we do not, we have no part of Jesus, just like Jesus told Peter - verse 8.

Jesus also told His disciples to follow His example and do the same to their brethren. Yes, this passage has always been interpreted as being humble, and doing acts of service for one another. However, I believe the meaning is much deeper.

Sometimes we need to help our brethren to clean the worldly mud off themselves. No, it does not mean berating them, or making them feel even more guilt and shame. It's in encouraging them to walk in the Spirit and keep step with Him.

> "*I say then: Walk in the Spirit, and you shall not fulfill the lust of the flesh.*" - **Galatians 5:16 NKJV**

It's encouraging them in the reading and studying of the word of God and in intimacy with Him.

> "*Your word I have hidden in my heart, that I might not sin against You.*" - **Psalm 119:11 NKJV**

Other times we really need to listen to the prompting of the Holy Spirit, with regards to our brother or sister in Christ, as He provides the exact help for us to give them: something tailored to their exact needs. The Holy Spirit may ask you to become their sounding board, or accountability partner if it involves some kind of addiction, and it may be for the long haul. It may be constant and deep intercession for them, and there may even be sacrifice required on your part. This is truly washing each other's feet!

Worldly filth separates us from God and impairs our relationship with Him. He wants us to go deeper in our love relationship with Him to ensure our faith is built up, our lamps are brightly burning, and we are ready and waiting for His return. He just wants our hearts. Everything else we follow when we truly love.

It is no longer a small fledgling church as in Acts, but a global people whom have made themselves ready - a spotless bride that Jesus desires to take to His home. It will be the Holy Spirit who will help her dress in holiness and righteousness, ready for her Groom. However, without a close and clean walk that is in step with the Holy Spirit, can we even have the *faith* to navigate the dark world in these end times, let alone have faith in His protection and the fulfilment of His so needed promises?

There is no longer the luxury of time to straighten things out. It will be the wise virgins who have trimmed their lamps with the oil of intimacy, (and who have plenty of the oil in reserve), that will enter in the now opened door, when the cry goes out that the Bridegroom is coming soon.

In that parable, when the cry went out that the Bridegroom was approaching, all the virgins trimmed their lamps. Who were the foolish virgins? They were also Christians. Their lamps were once burning brightly and they eagerly awaited Jesus' return, but in the end, their lights looked like petering out before He arrived, and they had nothing in reserve. The wise ones rightly told them to go and buy some more oil (for us that means going to where the anointing of intimacy resides – at church, in worship services, in personal prayer and in reading of the word, and so on.)

However, it takes time to develop our relationship with Him, and once on that band wagon of sin, it can be difficult to jump off. Only true repentance (turning away from the sin) and seeking God's forgiveness can rectify the problem. Even then we may have a long, hard slog to unlearn what has become habitual activities and thought patterns, and rebuild our faith in God.

If the Lord tarries and there remains enough time, going deeper in our love relationship with God will ensure our faith is built up, sin is kept at bay, our lamps are brightly burning, and we are ready and waiting for His return. This then is a matter of urgency not complacency.

Those that do not have the oil of intimacy, will no longer have time to change their situation. The door will slam fast, and even though they may consider that their hearts are now ready, they will not be allowed to enter. Instead, those latecomers will say on that day,

> "*Lord, Lord, have we not prophesied in Your name, cast out demons in Your name, and done many wonders in Your name?" but the Lord will declare to them, "I never knew you; depart from Me, you who practice lawlessness!*" - **Matthew 7:22-23 NKJV**

As I have previously discussed, it's not the fact that we have and can operate the gifts of the Holy Spirit that makes us holy, but that we demonstrate our love and faith in God through intimacy, obedience and acts of love. The gifts and callings are irrevocable! (Romans 11:29). They are gifts we can use, not spirituality yardsticks. Further they will pass away when we enter paradise.

> "*Love never fails. But whether there are prophecies, they will fail; whether there are tongues, they will cease; whether there is knowledge, it will vanish away.*" – **1 Corinthians 13:8 NKJV**

God will not be listening to those who use them as a reason to let them into paradise. Only those whose hearts are truly known to Him through a close relationship with Him – i.e., those that truly know Him. If we are still sinning and/or not drawing close to God, we are merely playing church and fooling ourselves, and this in itself, demonstrates the true state of our heart.

That sounds harsh, and many people reading this will no doubt object saying,

> "*Aren't we under grace though?*"

Although a discussion on grace will take me off topic completely, it's sufficed to say that we *are* under grace to the extent that our mistakes can be forgiven when we a repent, (i.e. making a firm decision to turn from doing those things and not do them again). In fact, there is a *throne* of grace which we can approach boldly to obtain mercy and help in our time of need. That's how big His grace is towards us. However, continual and *willful* sin is another story. Firstly continual sin not only demonstrates a lack desire to give up the sin, but also a lack of real repentance each time we front up to seek grace and forgiveness. Secondly, if a person continues in sin and disobedience, what does that say about their relationship with God? (See 1 John 1: 5-10 below)

> "*This is the message which we have heard from Him and declare to you, that God is light and in Him is no darkness at all. If we say that we have fellowship with Him, and walk in darkness, we lie and do not practice the truth. But if we walk in the light as He is in the light, we have fellowship with one another, and the blood of Jesus Christ His Son cleanses us from all sin.*
>
> *"If we say that we have no sin, we deceive ourselves, and the truth is not in us. If we confess our sins, He is faithful and just to forgive us our sins and to cleanse us from all unrighteousness. If we say that we have not sinned, we make Him a liar, and His word is not in us.*"
> – **1 John 1:5-10 NKJV**

If we truly love God, we will want to please Him. We will not want to do those things because we no longer desire to do them – our minds have been renewed by the word of God (Romans 12:2) and we now have the mind of Christ (1 Corinthians 2:16). Further, we have been transformed into His image because our eyes/focus is always upon Him. (1

Corinthians 3:18). This is what builds up our faith in Him.

Faith is built on the foundation of our intimacy and personal knowledge of God. It will be active more and more, as we yield to Him and draw close on His terms, not ours. Further, our intimacy and love will be obvious by our obedience to Him, our actions and attitudes towards others, and will ultimately manifest in greater faith and hope.

Conversely, disobedience puts distance between us and God, and dwindles our knowledge and understanding of Him. Willfulness and disobedience are also proof of a lack of real love in our hearts. Paul says that only these three things will last forever: faith hope and love, but the greatest of these is love, (1 Corinthians 13:13). **Love is the key that unlocks the faith and hope!** Without love we have *nothing* of eternal consequence, even faith!

Entanglement

What exactly is entanglement? It's when a small decision (whether by bad choices or an innocent mistake) can end up tying us down to worldly things, and as a result our attention and heart is no longer on Jesus, but that worldly thing in which we are entangled. And make no mistake, it is draining the love for God out of your heart, and the oil from your lamps.

Why do we become entangled? The move can be motivated simply by curiosity, like a sheep wandering over to something that's caught its attention, only to get caught in a thorny thicket while it's standing close to it, and as it tries to free itself, it becomes even more entangled. Entanglements can also happen when we foolishly decide, "*Oh, I can do this quickly and then leave this alone*", but later you may find you cannot let it go.

As well as curiosity, it may begin as an interest, but can quickly become obsession and then even addiction. Of course, not all entanglements are addictions. But anything that takes your attention away from God has the potential to entangle you. Thus, things like sports, cars, computer tech, TV shows, phones, video games, social media, or some other interest can take over a person's thinking and heart.

The more we try to break free on our own the deeper we fall in. It's like quicksand. If you struggle you sink faster. That's if in our own strength we decide we've had enough and leave it, but then succumb to temptations later, the obsession/addiction is now ramped up a level, making it more difficult to remove. (Think of the sheep analogy. It struggles to free itself, but the thorns only jab more the more it struggles.)

> "*For if, after they have escaped the pollutions of the world through the knowledge of the Lord and Savior Jesus Christ, they are again entangled in them and overcome, the latter end is worse for them than the beginning.*" – **2 Peter 2:20 – NKJV**

Christians are not immune! Anyone can fall into obsessions, and even addictions. Unfortunately, this is simply not talked about much from the pulpit on a Sunday. There are many of our brothers and sisters who are struggling alone for the shame of these things, and who really need help to be pulled out of the flames. They've made poor choices or walked blindly, innocently into the trap, and sometimes it only takes the one time and they're hooked.

I remember hearing the ex-prime-minister, Bob Hawk's

daughter testify about how her addiction to heroine started with one does some friends talked her into taking at a party. She said she knew that she was totally hooked from that time on. Porn and sex addicts sometimes say similar things. They found their dad's porn stash, or just happened to see someone changing through a window as they were walking past. A person might decide to have a "flutter" on the horses, or some other gamble, and after winning (it doesn't have to be a big win either), continue to gamble because they're looking for the exhilaration of the next win. One time is all it can take. It's a trap, a snare, and you're caught/entangled, and requires constant vigilance to prevent it from happening.

Nevertheless, after that first introduction, there is always a choice to do it again, and it is this choice to do it again, that I heard Jesus call "*foolishness*". Likewise, He called some other people foolish - the five foolish virgins. The foolish virgins had their hearts either divided or turned completely away to other things. Their heart lamps had no extra oil. Their love had cooled off. Unfortunately, they should never have looked away in the first place. They were foolish to choose those worldly things, and at such a critical time.

I remember hearing a pastor/counsellor once say that not all affairs of the heart are adultery as we think of it. In essence, anything or anyone that takes your attention, time and the love that would normally be given freely to your beloved, can be classified as adultery of the heart. Likewise, anyone or anything that takes your attention and heart away from Christ Jesus our husband, is spiritual adultery.

As I have previously stated, the more time we spend with God, the hungrier we become for Him. Likewise, the less time we spend, the more indifferent or dispassionate we are about spending time with Him. Therefore, if our time is dedicated to something else, more so than God, our hearts are already divided. You can't serve two masters. It then becomes easier from that point, for the enemy to entice you to spend more time doing something you enjoy doing, than to be disciplined and spend time with the one we need to be spending time with and who has our future in His hands. In the end it comes down to, '*Who or what really has our heart?*' We are in danger of committing spiritual adultery, and our heart lamps begin to dim.

Think of it, Jesus only did what He saw the Father do. Likewise, He expects us to do only those things He shows us, or the Holy Spirit guides us to do. This is sometimes easier said than done, but anything that is not sanctioned by God, has the potential to become a trap or snare. Remember how Jesus warned us:

> "*Many will say to Me in that day, 'Lord, Lord, have we not prophesied in Your name, cast out demons in Your name, and done many wonders in Your name?' And then I will declare to them, 'I never knew you; depart from Me, you who practice lawlessness!'*" – **Matthew 7:22-23 NKJV**

Doing our own good ideas are insufficient. We need to be doing God ideas. This is why, as sheep, we need a Good Shepherd to direct us and lead us to safer pastures, away from those supposedly "good ideas". Only following our Shepherd can keep us from becoming entangled.

Even so, Paul warns us to stand fast in our salvation freedom, and not to be enticed.

> "*Stand fast therefore in the liberty by which Christ has*

> *made us free, and do not be entangled again with a yoke of bondage.*" – **Galatians 5:1 NKJV**

The ESV calls it "***submitting*** *again to a yoke of* ***slavery***." In reality it's a battle for our very soul, and we must remain vigilant!

> "*No one engaged in warfare entangles himself with the affairs of this life, that he may please him who enlisted him as a soldier.*" – **2 Timothy 2:4 NKJV**

That's all very well and good, but no one sets out to become entangled. It's a trap designed just for you. That's right! I'm not here to pass judgement. We can all fall prey to this. So, after we have fallen into it, how can we emerge from entanglement unscathed?

Firstly, we need to recognise the situation for what it is: We're entangled. Addicts will need to admit they are addicted – even psychology says the first step to healing is realising there is in fact, a problem.

Then, the next step is to make a **decision**, a choice, to do something about it, even though the heart may be screaming that it doesn't want to stop, but if you wait for the desire to stop before you decide to do so, you won't ever stop. I heard an addict once say, "*Oh, I can give this up anytime I want to, but at the moment, I don't want to.*" While the heart rules, the decision to fix the problem will never come. So, here is where dying to self/flesh comes in. We must do what we know is right, despite how we merely "*feel*" about it.

Once you have firmly decided in your mind (and no, your flesh may *still* not be in agreement with that decision), we must cut off any access to going back to that interest / obsession / addiction. When I asked Jesus how to be free, I heard Jesus say, "*Cut the head off the serpent!*" The enemy that has lured and enticed you to that place, and has wrapped himself around you like a coiling serpent. The more you struggle, the tighter he holds on. **BUT** Jesus has overcome the enemy of your soul and He alone is your way to freedom. So, cut the head off the serpent! Get rid of the things that caused you to start, then the reminders and triggers. Be strong! Fight against your feelings for it is truly a battle for your soul.

However, this is only the beginning. Becoming *un*tangled is never a quick process, nor is it easy. When a sheep becomes entangled in the thorny thicket, it takes some time to remove all the thorny branches without tearing the flesh of the sheep. All that time the sheep is crying out in pain and moving around trying to make it stop. The Shepherd has to pacify the sheep and hold it still while in cuts it free.

Likewise, it can be a painful process for us to remove our entanglements. Though there may be an instance when people are set free immediately in a prayer line, most people who are entangled have to do the hard yards. If the entanglement has moved on from obsession to addiction, the way out is to be far more difficult, but the principles are the same.

The biggest problem we face at this juncture in time in the church age, is that time is running out. The church Age is at its closure and Jesus will soon return to begin a new age with His Millennial Reign. Therefore, we can no longer afford to just "let things go", the way they have always been. The call has gone out, "*The Bridegroom is on His way!*" Remember the foolish virgins tried to find more oil quickly, but by the time they came back, it was too late for them, and the door was closed to them. Becoming untangled takes time and tenacious persistence. Then it takes more time to actually renew your relationship with God. His love has never left you, but your heart has cooled off and needs renewal.

This is not just about forming new habits but breaking a strong spiritual net that has enclosed around you and sucked the love you once had for the Master, from your heart. You may even feel that since you no longer have the passion you once had for God, that there's little to motivate you to break free. Don't be fooled by this evil argument based on mere feelings of the flesh. If we are entangled, we really have only two choices: Get rid of the entanglement as quickly as possible, or lose your Godly eternity.

In fact, Jesus told His disciples about sin and those who go astray in Matthew 18, that when we are caught in sin, sometimes we have no option but to bite the bullet and deal with it.

> "*If your hand or foot causes you to sin, cut it off and cast it from you. It is better for you to enter into life lame or maimed, rather than having two hands or two feet, to be cast into the everlasting fire. And if your eye causes you to sin, pluck it out and cast it from you. It is better for you to enter into life with one eye, rather than having two eyes, to be cast into hell fire.*
>
> *"Take heed that you do not despise one of these little ones, for I say to you that in heaven their angels always see the face of My Father who is in heaven. For the Son of Man has come to save that which was lost.*
>
> *"What do you think? If a man has a hundred sheep, and one of them goes astray, does he not leave the ninety-nine and go to the mountains to seek the one*

> *that is straying? "And if he should find it, assuredly, I say to you, he rejoices more over that sheep than over the ninety-nine that did not go astray. Even so it is not the will of your Father who is in heaven that one of these little ones should perish."* – **Matthew 18:8-14 NKJV**

Firstly, Jesus doesn't pull any punches. He tells it like it is. It's going to hurt cutting off those things in which we've become entangled. Just like cutting off your hand!

Then He tells the rest of the brethren to not look down on those who are entangled and who feel like they are the least in the Kingdom (the little ones – note He didn't change the subject mid-stream).

Then, Jesus continues to explain that that once lost sheep is extremely valuable to Him, so much so that He is willing to leave the ninety-nine in a safe place and seek out that sheep that is lost. He is simply not willing to let you go and perish.

The Good Shepherd is right there to enable us to overcome, but it will take some effort and perhaps even persistent endurance, and a tenacious will power that declares "***No!***", because it is simply the right choice before God, even when every fibre of your physical and emotional being is screaming otherwise. It may have been your heart that caused you to become ensnared, but in some ways, it has to be your head that must take control over the flesh to bring it back and discipline it. Following God's will is always that logical choice. The flesh must submit!

The good news is according to Paul, we already have the weapons we need for our warfare, and that they are there to bring every thought/argument captive.

> "*For the weapons of our warfare are not carnal but mighty in God for pulling down strongholds, casting down arguments and every high thing that exalts itself against the knowledge of God, bringing every thought into captivity to the obedience of Christ, and being ready to punish all disobedience when your obedience is fulfilled.*" – **2 Corinthians 10:4-6 NKJV**

The flesh may be trying to convince you that you need this, or a little won't hurt, or just once more, but that is a lie, an argument that needs to be pulled down. Also just knowing that Jesus is beside you and helping and strengthening you, can enable you, with spiritual grit determination, to continue. When we look to Him, and when we walk in step with the Holy Spirit, we will give no provision for the flesh.

> "*I say then: Walk in the Spirit, and you shall not fulfill the lust of the flesh.*" – **Galatians 5:16 NKJV**

> "*But put on the Lord Jesus Christ, and make no provision for the flesh, to fulfill its lusts.*" – **Romans 13:14 NKJV**

Know this, however, the enemy is not going to simply stop. He will continue to entice you, and he knows exactly what buttons to push. Nevertheless, don't give in and yield to the temptation. Stick with your decision, for the Lord is with you.

> "*Not by might nor by power, but by My Spirit,' says the Lord of hosts.*" – **Zechariah 4:6b NKJV**

It's all about turning your eyes to Jesus – the Good Shepherd and asking for His help.

You might be thinking, but I keep thinking about it. There's something wrong with me. Doubtful! Those thoughts are most likely **not yours**. Firstly, we have the mind of Christ.

> *"For "who has known the mind of the LORD that he may instruct Him?" But we have the mind of Christ."* – **1 Corinthians 2:16 NKJV**

When we are first saved, He gives us a new mind and heart. Our motivations are changed. Then we maintain our minds and renew them daily in the word

> *"And do not be conformed to this world, but be transformed by the renewing of your mind, that you may prove what is that good and acceptable and perfect will of God."* - **1 Corinthians 12:2 NKJV**

We begin to think like Jesus, we understand His character, those things that please Him, and the things He is likely to say. Thus, we recognise our Good Shepherd's voice.

In reality, there are three possible origins of the voices that Christians hear:

1) Our thoughts,

2) thoughts from God, or

3) thoughts from the evil one.

Human thoughts logically progress from one thing to the next. That line of thought may have commenced because of something we saw or experienced or something that was said and that in turn brought up memories, or other associated thoughts, but always there is a progression.

When a thought comes at you out of the blue – you may not have even been thinking about anything remotely related to it - it usually has a spiritual origin. So, how can we tell if it's of God or a demon?

If we are well versed in the word of God, we will know that God will never contradict His word, (He never lies, so we can trust with absolutely certainty that His Word is true, and therefore, no adjustments, revisions or amendments are required. There's no reason for Him to do so, ever!) Neither will the words He speaks contradict the character of God. Does the word you just heard sound like something God would say? What are the ramifications and therefore, fruits of this, if it is really God's voice? Will it hurt others?

If you are unsure about this, when God speaks to you, there is a quiet peaceful acknowledgement on your behalf that agrees with what He said. It is reasonable, and doesn't evoke any negative reactions at all in your spirit.

Conversely, if the enemy fires a fiery dart at us, it carries the fuel of emotion, enough to explode into a raging fire which is hard to ignore. These thoughts will eventually give birth to actions, which definitely bear bad fruit. These thoughts can also cause you to act impulsively, not stopping to think about the consequences of what you are about to do, or whether it is right or wrong. You just want to do it now. The manipulation of emotions is a quick and sneaky way the enemy uses to entice you to do things you would not normally do, and without giving it much thought before you do.

Having said that, if an enticing thought suddenly drops into your mind out of nowhere, we must first ask ourselves, who is it coming from? You thought it was your thoughts, but if we have the mind of Christ, unless you were doing something that merely reminded you of your entanglement, (triggers are another issue), those thoughts are coming from the enemy. When you realise this, even psychology studies in this area agree that you have about a split second to make a choice to stop thinking about it, otherwise you will fall back into your obsession/addiction. If you continue to think about it, the enemy has you, and the dart ignites your passions into a raging fire.

Unfortunately, retreating on its own as a combat strategy, is insufficient. We also need other tools to ensure we stand firm. Praise be to God, Jesus gave us the perfect example of what to do. What did He do when He was tempted in the wilderness? He countered the attack with the word of God.

Let's take a closer look at this. What did He say when the enemy tempted him with gratification of the flesh, Jesus countered by quoted Scripture (Deuteronomy 8:3):

> "*But He answered and said, "It is written, 'Man shall not live by bread alone, but by every word that proceeds from the mouth of God.'*"" – **Matthew 4:4 NKJV**

He'd rather remain hungry in the flesh, as uncomfortable as that may have been, and instead have His eternal Spirit nourished by His Father's words, than to gratify his flesh. Note, had Jesus yielded, He would have been agreeing to do the will of the devil. It was Adam and Eve that made that same mistake in the garden. Now Jesus, as the second Adam, as a man, was taking back that authority and giving it back to His Father!

When Satan then suggested He display His Kingly authority and power by jumping off the temple in front pf everyone to prove it, how did Jesus respond? His Father, wouldn't allow Him to die before His time. However, Jesus knew the plan of the Father better than anyone. It was to be persecuted by the very ones with whom God had entrusted the laws, and then to die a sacrificial death so that the debt of sin could be paid and claimed by any who would allow Him to infuse Himself to them and submit their lives to Him as a new clean and purified creation. Thus, He was not about to yield to Satan's will and do something which was not part of His father's will. He only did what He saw the Father did, and was not about to "test" God to see if He would live up to that prophetic promise. He already had **absolute faith** in what His Father could do, and would do. Thus, Jesus countered by quoting Deuteronomy 6:16.

> "*Jesus said to him, 'It is written again, 'You shall not tempt the LORD your God.'?*" – **Matthew 4:7 NKJV**

Then the devil offered Him all the wealth and power of the entire earth, - complete power over every nation and kingdom, if He would just worship him. (Just as an aside here: If He had become ruler of the world under Satan, He still wouldn't really be in control but under his master's absolute control, not doing whatever He wanted but still on a leash. Nor would those things that satan claimed were his and had promised to give Him, really be His, for the same reason. He would have still been under the master's control, and he would have made Him use those things for His own will and purposes. See how empty Satan's words are. At any rate, the world is the Lord's and all the fulness thereof, and Jesus will take claim to it legitimately when He returns.)

Returning to our point, Jesus again answered this temptation with Scripture (Deuteronomy 6:13)

> "*Then Jesus said to him, "Away with you, Satan! For it is written, 'You shall worship the LORD your God, and Him only you shall serve.'?""* – **Matthew 4:10 NKJV**

What does that look like for us when temptation comes calling? Firstly, as mentioned, we need recognise whose voice we are hearing. Then we need to make a split-second decision to say "*No!*" Then we pull out our active two edge sword to slices right to the root and exposes the lies in the light of His absolute truth, (Hebrews 4:12).

It looks like: "*No! Be gone, Satan! I rebuke you,*" followed by, "*It is written...*" Of course, this also presupposes that we are armed with the particular Scriptures that deal with our temptations.

Paul in his letter to the Ephesians, also makes this obvious. This is a well-known passage of Scripture and you can no doubt recite it off by heart:

> "*Finally, my brethren, be strong in the Lord and in the power of His might. Put on the whole armour of God, that you may be able to stand against the wiles of the devil. For we do not wrestle against flesh and blood, but against principalities, against powers, against the rulers of the darkness of this age, against spiritual hosts of wickedness in the heavenly places. Therefore, take up the whole armour of God, that you may be able to withstand in the evil day, and having done all, to stand.*
>
> *Stand therefore, having girded your waist with* ***truth****, having put on the breastplate of* ***righteousness****, and having shod your feet with the* ***preparation of the gospel of peace****; above all, taking the* ***shield of faith*** *with which you will be able to quench all the fiery darts of the wicked one. And take the* ***helmet of salvation****, and the* ***sword of the Spirit****, which is the word of God;* ***praying always*** *with all prayer and supplication in the Spirit, being watchful to this end with all perseverance and supplication for all the saints.*" – **Ephesians 6:10-18 NKJV**

A Christians lifestyle must be based on truth, and righteousness, and with readiness to share the gospel. These are the things that help us to stand firmly and unashamedly in the time of trial. If we fail in these areas, it gives the enemy a legal right to begin hurting us.

When we are under attack with those fiery darts, we stand in our faith and trust in God. We know to whom we truly belong, and subsequently, stand firm on our salvation. This salvation is not shaky – here today and gone tomorrow – but based on what Jesus has done – a fact written in eternity. Yep, we have all made mistakes, but like the prodigal son, have been accepted back and forgiven no matter what our feelings or circumstances are trying to tell us. Further, God will never abandon us, leave us or forsake us. Our salvation is strong and secure despite what lies the enemy is spinning about us.

We then cut through the enemy's lies with the sword of the Spirit, which is the word of God, speaking His truth, a truth which the enemy cannot deny, and dissolving his lofty negativity and accusations.

Finally, we pray for ourselves and for our brethren that we can be watchful of the enemy's advances, and have the perseverance to continue in prayer. We must still remain vigilant, because he can hit you at any time. The temptations will still come at you out of the blue, but will become less the more we resist.

> "*Therefore, submit to God. Resist the devil and he will flee from you.*" – **James 4:7 NKJV**

Even though we may be free, it is still easy to fall back into bad habits, but the Word of God states that if we hide ourselves under the shadow of His wings, He will deliver us from the snare of the fowler.

> "*Surely He shall deliver you from the snare of the fowler and from the perilous pestilence.*" – **Psalm 91:3 ESV**

He will never abandon you. He is completely faithful to His love and covenant to you. However, the reason most people are not freed from their entanglement, is because they struggle alone for the shame of asking for help, and then failing time and again, they give up trying. Instead of hiding under the shadow of His wing, they remain in fear of reprisal under the banner of shame.

In saying this, you may feel like you've blown it far beyond help. You may even hear the enemy constantly insist that you've gone too far and that God is now beyond your reach, and even if you were to cry out, He wouldn't want such a horrible sinner and unfaithful servant back. These are all lies!

I will say again: He is not willing that you should perish. You are valuable to Him – enough to die for you in the first place. His love is not here today and gone tomorrow. It's not like, "one mistake and you're out!", but is long suffering towards us. His love for you is so enormous, it's almost beyond our comprehension. That's why Paul prays that

> "*For this reason I bow my knees to the Father of our Lord Jesus Christ, from whom the whole family in heaven and earth is named, that He would grant you, according to the riches of His glory, to be strengthened with might through His Spirit in the inner man, that Christ may dwell in your hearts through faith; that you, being rooted and grounded in love, may be able to* ***comprehend with all the saints what is the width***

> ***and length and depth and height — to know the love of Christ which passes knowledge****; that you may be filled with all the fullness of God.*
>
> *"Now to Him who is* ***able to do exceedingly abundantly above all that we ask or think****, according to the power that works in us, to Him be glory in the church by Christ Jesus to all generations, forever and ever. Amen."* – **Ephesians 3:14-21 NKJV**

He loves you *exceedingly* abundantly, so much so that we need our inner man strengthened just to be able to comprehend it and even then, we may take an eternity to discover it's enormity. He is also able to do far more than we ask or think. He is in batting for you. He understands your problem, but He also wants you to know that you can become untangled. He has even provided a way of escape for you. In fact, Paul tells the Corinthians,

> "***No temptation*** *has overtaken you except such as is common to man; but God is faithful, who* ***will not allow you to be tempted beyond what you are able****, but with the temptation will also* ***make the way of escape****, that you may be able to bear it."* – **1 Corinthians 10:13 NKJV**

The word also states that, **I can do all things through Christ who strengthens me**. (Philippians 4:13) As the saying goes, "It ain't over until it's over!" It's a battle with evil forces for your very soul, and that battle may be fierce, but you can overcome because you have the Good Shepherd, and He has already overcome. You are not alone!

> *"Let us therefore come boldly to the throne of grace, that we may obtain mercy and find grace to help in time of need."* – **Hebrews 4:16 NKJV**

Many have looked at that verse and thought it's merely about petitioning God for something we need, like a new job, or money to pay the bills or for healing etc., but this verse carries so much more. The verse speaks of "**mercy**" and "**help**" in our time of need. If you're struggling in entanglement, you are in a time of need. You need help and His great mercy. Therefore, don't stay under shame. You are still His child, and you can boldly and unashamedly, ask the Father for His mercy and His help to become untangled, and again walking with Him.

He wants us to be fully looking to Him, and drawing close to Him so that our heart lamps are constantly being fuelled by His love, and thus, our faith in Him will also rise.

Unforgiveness

In my first book, "*Save Your Marriage: How to Restore & Rebuild a Christian Marriage on the Precipice of Divorce*", I dedicated an entire chapter on this topic, which included much of the scientific research conducted on the subject. Suffice to say, I will not be repeating that here, but will try to include the main points, and some exerts.

It has been proven that the hurts that we encounter are worst when we have invested much of our lives and time and love into a particular person. If an acquaintance did something similar, it wouldn't phase us. This much is self-evident. However, once we are hurt, suddenly we feel as if all that we have been giving into that relationship has not counted for anything and the one who hurt us now *owes* us, at least an apology or explanation. Some may even feel angry, ripped off, and want to "get even". Actually, anger is quite often the reflex action that wells up as a defence mechanism. Subconsciously, you do not want the emotional pain, and so direct that via anger, back on the one hurting you.

However, unless we deal with the hurt and forgive as Jesus has instructed us, there will be great fallout both spiritually and physically. Yes, you read that correctly. Unforgiveness has been proven to make you physically sick, and the longer you hold on to it, the worse the conditions become.

The medical link between unforgiveness and disease has been well researched and documented, and these results can be found in many books and papers that have been recently published. Below I have included just a few people's conclusions to such research:

The latest research (Elliott 2011[7]) has yielded this conclusion:

> "*Over an extended period of time, unforgiveness can be experienced as negative emotions that result in a cascade of biological and brain responses. Findings about the body's hormone response to unforgiveness reveal that unforgiveness is reflected in specific cortisol levels, adrenaline production and cytokine balance (Worthington et al 2005) with patterns that parallel those reported in people living with high stress. These hormone patterns are known to compromise the immune system (Berry and Worthington 2001; Seybold et al. 2001) with the long-term consequence of leading to several identified chronic illnesses (Danese et al 2007).*"

Dr Michael Barry – author of "*The Forgiveness Project*" made this comment:

---

7 By Barbara Elliot, "*Forgiveness Therapy: A Clinical Intervention for Chronic Disease*" 2011. Journal of Religion and Health, 50(2), 240-247

"Harbouring these negative emotions, this anger and hatred, creates a state of chronic anxiety. Chronic anxiety very predictably produces adrenalin and cortisol, which in turn deplete the production of natural killer cells which are your body's foot-soldiers in the fight against cancer."[8]

Dr. David Servan-Schrieber, MD, Anti-Cancer stated:

"Inwardly, the emotional wound affects deep vital processes. A psychological wound sets off mechanisms of the stress response...release of cortisol, adrenaline... (including) a slowdown in the immune system... ... which contributes to growth and spread of cancer."

There is no denying the facts that unforgiveness causes serious illness in the body, but more importantly, unforgiveness causes spiritual illness as well. If we do not forgive, not only is our relationship with brethren in jeopardy, but so is our relationship with God.

"For if you forgive other people when they sin against you, your heavenly Father will also forgive you. 15 But if you do not forgive others their sins, your Father will not forgive your sins." -**Matthew 6:14-15 NIV**

Again, in Mark's gospel:

"And when you stand praying, if you hold anything against anyone, forgive them, so that your Father in heaven may forgive you your sins." **Mark 11:25 NIV**

For the Christian, forgiveness is not merely an option - it was commanded, and as much as seventy times seven.

---

8 Dr. Michael S Barry, "*The Forgiveness Project*", Published by Kregel Publications 2011

Further to this, at the end of the parable of the unforgiving servant, Jesus makes this statement:

> "*And his master was angry, and delivered him to the torturers until he should pay all that was due to him. 35 So My heavenly Father also will do to you if each of you, from his heart, does not forgive his brother his trespasses.*" – **Matthew 18:35-35 NKJV**

Firstly, I'd like to point out that the Master in this parable was extremely *angered* by the servant's unforgiveness. God has given up His Son as a sacrifice for sin, because He so loved us. How can we then, being forgiven and made a new creation that looks like Him, not do the same in turn? By not forgiving as He did for us, we are in fact, making light of the love and cost He paid, and elevating ourselves above our master. As His disciples, we should like exactly like Jesus (a "disciple" is one who trains to look exactly like the master.)

Secondly, the reference to the "torturers" (the Greek word is "*basanistes*" [Strong's 930], is better translated as "*tormentor*".) It is not referring to hell and damnation after we die, as some would suppose (though that might be the finality of it if someone was not ever willing to forgive). The unforgiving servant had himself, already been forgiven by God, (or if you follow the analogy through - saved by grace, washed clean and made fully righteous).

Jesus's point here concerns God's sons and daughters who refuse to obey the command to forgive just as they have been forgiven. We don't like to talk about the discipline and chastisement of God but it is real none the less, for we are even told that the Father disciplines those whom He loves. (Hebrews 12:5b-6)

What then does it mean to be delivered to the tormenters? What does that look like for us? Remember what happened to King Saul when God chastised him: God left him at the mercy of tormenting spirits to send a message to Saul to change his attitude, (1 Samuel 18:7-10.) The torturers were tormenting spirits. They may torment the mind, or the physical body, i.e. infirmities. The meaning of the parable is, therefore, obvious: if you choose not to forgive, you will be left at the mercy of tormenting spirits until you do.

Please note: God is not causing these inflictions nor tormenting you Himself. It is sin that separates us from God, and the further removed from Him in love, the less we experience His loving protection. (Psalm 91 tells us that it is under the shadow of His wing – the place of intimacy – that we find His protection.) This distance allows the tormenters free access that God does not deny (they actually have legal access because of our refusal to obey God), in order that we learn, not just that He is displeased, but that there are severe consequences to our willful sin. Added to that, the more separated from God we are, the harder it is for us to hear God's voice and to stand in faith. In fact, I would go so far as to restate that sin is a destroyer of faith, and unforgiveness is such a sin.

Further, God is serious about our attitudes towards each other – especially in the area of unforgiveness. God is a God of restoration, love and unity. He is motivated by His complete and utterly passionate love towards each one of us. As such, to allow any rift between His children would be incongruent to that love. Unforgiveness prevents restoration and continues to hurt each person the longer it festers.

Thirdly, As New Creations in Christ, it is no longer I that lives but Christ who lives in me. Likewise, Christ lives in the one who hurt you. To exercise unforgiveness and even bitterness towards them is to do so to Christ, Himself. Jesus makes this clear when He describes the judgement of the nations:

> "*Assuredly, I say to you, inasmuch as you did it to one of the least of these My brethren, you did it to Me.*" - **Matthew 25:40 NKJV**

> "*Assuredly, I say to you, inasmuch as you did not do it to one of the least of these, you did not do it to Me.*" - **Matthew 25: 45 NKJV**

No longer is the command simply to love your neighbour as yourself. Jesus gave us a *new* commandment: (John 13:34) that we love one another as He loves us – i.e. completely and unconditionally. The benchmark is no longer how much we can love ourselves, and therefore others, but how much Christ who lives in us, can love through us.

This means that forgiveness is given without expectation of an apology or any condition at all, just as He demonstrated at the cross. "*Father, forgive them for they know not what they do.*" He did not say, "*If they are truly sorry and ask to be forgiven then I'll forgive them.*" No, He gave His forgiveness without condition to those who did not deserve it, nor were they repentant. In fact, they were still hurling abuse at Him while He hung there!!

This was not the only moment that Jesus forgave in this manner. When a bunch of people lowered the paralytic down through the hole in the roof, Jesus told him that his sins were forgiven, (Matthew 9:2-8; Mark 2:1-12; Luke 5:17-26). The man hadn't asked for forgiveness at all. Rather, he had come seeking healing! When the religious became offended at this, Jesus reminded them that it was harder to forgive (and heal emotionally) than to heal a physical ailment, but to prove to them He was God and could do both, Jesus healed the man as well.

Jesus also forgave the woman caught in adultery, (John 8:1-11). After the crowd left on conviction of their own sinfulness, He asked the woman where all her accusers were – was there no one left to condemn her. The woman confirmed there was no one left. Jesus then responded, "*Neither do I condemn you. Go and sin no more!*"

It's safe to say she knew she was guilty and deserved death under the laws of this people. Like most, she would, in the very least, have been sorry she had been caught and left to bear the full consequences of her sins. However, she hadn't asked Jesus for forgiveness or even mercy, nor was there recorded in John's gospel any demonstration of remorse or repentance on her part. Nevertheless, Jesus gave her forgiveness freely.

As He is, so are we in this world (1 John 4:17b). As you have been freely given forgiveness, so freely give, (Matthew 10:8). The call to forgive is not only to forgive those who ask to be forgiven, though that is definitely the case as well, (see Matthew 18:21-22), as Christians we must love as Christ loves and forgive as He forgives. Moreover, if we do not forgive from our hearts, we risk chastisement for disobedience.

To forgive your brethren for any hurt they have caused is not only the first step to your own reconciliation, but also your own spiritual health. It doesn't matter whether they are sorry or not. In fact, there may be plethora of other arguments as to why you shouldn't forgive, despite the Biblical command to do so. Most of these arguments, however, revolve around common myths concerning forgiveness, and as such need to be addressed outright:

* Forgiveness is **not** reconciliation.

* Forgiveness does **not** deny responsibility, condone or excuse the behaviour of the offender, nor does stop the pursuit of justice.

* Forgiving does **not** invalidate the fact that the victim has been hurt. The hurt may not even be gone when you're ready to forgive. Damage and wounds take time to repair.

* It does **not** mean that the victim will forget. Rather, once the negative emotions have been released, the victim is free to revisit the past without being harmed again by it.

No one is suggesting this is an easy task, nor did Jesus, but it can be done because it is no longer I who live but Christ who lives in me, and this life I live by faith in the Son of God! (Galatians 2:20) If Jesus can forgive even unto death, that same Christ in me enables me to forgive as well. I can personally attest to the power of this in my own life. I know He is able to help you do the same.

You may have taken the issue to the feet of Jesus several times, and still the hurt wells up to haunt you, making you believe you cannot forgive that person. Firstly, let me state that when you take the situation to God, and genuinely tell Him that you forgive that person, the transaction is considered finished. It's done and dusted. At that point we have given to God our "right" to pay them back or punish them for their hurtful actions. Now it's in God's hands, not ours. What remains with us, however, is the hurt and emotional fallout that requires working through and/or healing. In order to recover from the really deep hurts, we may even require the Holy Spirits help. This doesn't mean you have not forgiven. It simply means you are still feeling and dealing with the hurt.

This is especially difficult when the infraction is ongoing over a period of time, and we are therefore required to give constant forgiveness to them each time they take another stab at us, whether they are repentant or not. However, forgiving them is for your sake – not theirs. God will deal with them in His own way, but He expects us to forgive regardless of what happens to them from that point on.

This doesn't mean you put yourself back into an abusive situation, especially if it is more than verbal, (in fact, if you're in harm's way, you may have to be completely removed from the situation), but it does mean you are not clinging to the problem, reliving every moment again and again, or trying to figure out ways to get even, or even rehearse would you will say to them if you see them again. Forgiveness means you leave the incident, with all its hurts and bruises, at Jesus feet, and allow Him to heal your hurts. You may even need Christian counselling if you simply can't deal with it. Emotional wounding can be very deep, but still we are expected to be like Jesus, and forgive others.

Unforgiveness is one of those dirty dishes that need to be washed off, otherwise it will not be mould growing there, but the roots of bitterness and they will destroy not only faith, but your relationship with Jesus, and your health as well.

Chapter 4
The Hope Factor

~~~~~~~~~~~~~~~

Hope is a close cousin to the Faith. However, without a Biblical understanding, you might be tempted to think that hope and faith are not cousins at all but rather the antithesis of each other. We quite often hear people say, "*Oh, I hope it happens!*" but they're not really convinced it will, in fact, occur. We are meant to be a people of faith and yet, if we merely hope something happens, doesn't that contradict faith? For the non-churched, "*yes*". This hope then would be an empty and *vain* hope.

However, for believers, faith and hope are obviously not the same as in the world. We know that Christians do *not* hope in vain, nor is our faith in vain. A reading of 1 Corinthians 15 will make this point very clear.

There is a difference between worldly hope and Biblical hope. To understand Biblical hope better, and how it interacts with faith, we must first investigate the Old Testament to discover how it portrays hope, and then to ascertain how that hope was understood by Jesus, the apostles, and indeed all of us under the New Covenant.

In the Old Covenant, God's chosen people had the Law of Moses, but not salvation in Christ. Does that mean they had no hope? Of course not! How then is their hope not in vain, especially in the light of 1 Corinthians 15? Why exactly did the children of Israel hope in God despite the troubles they faced? What was it that gave them confidence in the outcomes they hoped for? And do we have access to the same hope as Gentile believers?
~~~~~~~~~~~~~~~

Old Testament Hope

Abraham's Legacy

God was Israel's foundation of hope right from the time of its father, Abraham. Not only did Abraham have hope beyond hope that God's promise would supersede the natural state of things but those promises were fulfilled. Abraham,

> "*who, contrary to hope, in hope believed*" – **Romans 4:18 NKJV**

He knew God well enough to be called God's friend. He had unwavering confidence in who God was, His power and authority, and His truthfulness. God would do as He said He would do because He does not lie.

400 years after Abraham, God remembered His covenant to Abraham and rescued Abraham's offspring from under the lash of slavery.

> "*So, God heard their groaning, and God remembered His covenant with Abraham, with Isaac, and with Jacob.*" – **Exodus 2:24 NKJV**

What's more when He delivered them, He gave them all the spoils of Egypt, and led them to a land of milk and honey. Yes, they had to conquer the land, but He went before them in battle and brought about great and miraculous victories, time and time again. They witnessed His justice and judgement, but also His mercy and forgiveness. Because He is a Holy God, He frequently warned them, pleaded with them through His prophets, to come back to Him because of His great love for them. They understood that He was a personal God. Even the psalmists – especially David – testified of His intimate dealings with them.

Prisoners of Hope

The God of Israel wasn't like the gods of the pagan nations surrounding them, and who demanded human sacrifices in order to be appeased, and who could not be known on a personal level. To the nation of Israel, He was God who had bound Himself to them, for He intervened and protected them and always followed through with His promises to them. They knew that their God only spoke truth and was always true to His word. He was faithful and could not fail. They had witnessed this many, many times.

Thus, because they had witnessed God's character and faithfulness, and experienced His great love and power to save, the nation of Israel had a ***solid foundation*** on which they based their hopes. ***He*** was their **hope** for the future. ***He*** would fulfil all His promises to them. This hope was solid. Like a person in a prison, nothing could possibly enter their thinking to dissuade them from this hope.

In Zechariah 9:11–12, God promises to save His people and calls them ***prisoners of HOPE***:

> "[11] *As for you also, Because of the blood of your covenant, I will set your prisoners free from the waterless pit. 12 Return to the stronghold, You* ***prisoners of hope****. Even today I declare That I will restore double to you.*"
> - **Zechariah 9:11–12 NKJV**

A prison is a very secure place that a prisoner cannot leave and outsiders cannot enter. The hope of God's chosen people could not be penetrated, or polluted, or watered down. It was rock solid. This unshakeable hope in God even led the prophet Jeremiah, amidst his darkness time, to write in the Book of Lamentations,

> "[18]*And I said, "My strength and my hope have perished from the LORD."* [19] *Remember my affliction and roaming, The wormwood and the gall.* [20] *My soul still remembers and sinks within me.* [21]*This I recall to my mind. Therefore,* ***I have hope****.* [22]*Through the LORD's mercies we are not consumed, because His compassions fail not.* [23]*They are new every morning; Great is Your faithfulness.* [24]*"The LORD is my portion," says my soul,* ***"Therefore, I hope in Him!""*** - **Lamentations 3:18–24 NKJV**

Likewise, the Psalmist has witnessed how God has upheld him since birth, and so writes,

> "*For* ***You are my hope****, O Lord GOD; You are my trust from my youth.*" – **Psalm 71:5 NJKV**

Thus, we can positively say that Old Testament Hope was based on ***God's character***, who He was, the truth of His words, and also upon the evidence of the fulfilment of His promises, His intervention to save them, and the miracles He did on their behalf. These things they had witnessed several times over.

How then does that differ from New Testament hope, or is it really the same?

New Testament Hope

Now someone might be tempted to say,

> "*Yeah, but that was for the Jews. They'd lived through all that. We're under the New Covenant and besides, you don't know what I've been through. What hope is*

there for me?"

Well, you'd be wrong if you thought like that because, the apostle Paul makes it very clear in Romans that we have the same hope as the Israel did under the Old Covenant.

> "[8]*Now I say that Jesus Christ has become a servant to the circumcision for the truth of God, to confirm the promises made to the fathers, [9]and that the Gentiles might glorify God for His mercy, as it is written:*
>
> > *"For this reason, I will confess to You among the Gentiles, and sing to Your name." - (2 Samuel 22:50; Psalm 18:49)*
>
> [10]*And again he says:*
>
> > *"Rejoice, O Gentiles, with His people!" – (Deuteronomy 32:43)*
>
> [11]*And again:*
>
> > *"Praise the LORD, all you Gentiles! Laud Him, all you peoples!" – (Psalm 117:1)*
>
> [12]*And again, Isaiah says:*
>
> > *"There shall be a root of Jesse; And He who shall rise to reign over the Gentiles, In Him the Gentiles shall* ***hope****." – (Isaiah 11:10)*
>
> [13]*Now may the* ***God of hope*** *fill you with all joy and peace in believing, that you may abound in hope by the power of the Holy Spirit."* – **Romans 15:8-13 NKJV**

In other words, we as Gentiles have that same hope as the Jewish people did. That is, our hope is in God. What He says goes! He is the God of Hope, or the One who gives us hope. Further to that end, He has also given us the Holy Spirit who enables us to abound in hope.

God Does Not Lie!

In other words, there is more than enough hope/certainty that God will do as He said He would, to the point of overflow.

> "*God is not a man, that He should lie*" - **Numbers 23:19 NKJV**

If God said it, if it's in His word, then it's true and reliable!

We can be sure because God does not **need** to lie. He has no motivation to do so. Therefore, His words and promises are absolutely true and certain. When a person lies, it is usually to gain something: whether a person's or persons' praise, esteem, something from them, or to trick others for some kind of long-term gain, or to avoid punishment for doing something wrong; possibly even to shift blame in order to get off "Scott free". However, God doesn't need to do any of that. He is already seated in the highest place of glory, power and authority. He's already above all. Everything is subject to Him. He knows all, is the wisest and most loving God ever. He is already perfect and doesn't need to change to better Himself. Why would He need to lie? There is nothing for Him to gain (because He already has everything) and lying would only taint His already perfect character. There's absolutely no motivation for God to lie or give false hope. So, whatever God speaks is the absolute truth. He is truth! You can totally depend on it.

Therefore, this hope we have in His promised future is a certainty. It makes worldly hopes not worth chasing. In fact, nothing but His promises are worth holding on to. Why put our hopes in maybes and uncertainties. Even Paul warns the wealthy not to put their hope in uncertain riches but on God.

> "*As for the rich in this present age, charge them not to be haughty, nor to set their* ***hopes*** *on the uncertainty of riches, but on God, who richly provides us with everything to enjoy.*" – **1 Timothy 6:17 ESV**

Why? Because in God there is certainty, but riches are here today and gone tomorrow like shifting sands. Stuff happens in life and you can't predict it, but those who hope in God will always flourish.

> "*He who trusts in his riches will fall, but the righteous will flourish like foliage.*" – **Proverbs 11:28 NKJV**

Therefore, Paul says,

> "*For to this end we toil and strive, because we have our hope set on the living God, who is the Savior of all people, especially of those who believe.*" – **1 Timothy 4:10 ESV**

Paul was not toiling for wealth but for the Kingdom, despite the hardships that constantly befell him. However, he confidently set our hopes on Jesus. As such Paul was able to testify,

> "*He delivered us from such a deadly peril, and he will deliver us. On Him we have set our hope that he will deliver us again.*" - **2 Corinthians 1:10 ESV**

This is for us too. He will deliver us when things look darkest. The writer of Hebrews also encourages the readers with this same sentiment,

> "*Let us hold fast the confession of our hope without wavering, for he who promised is faithful.*" – **Hebrews 10:23 ESV**

We may face extreme disaster in the natural, but we hold onto our confession of hope in Him, for not only is He able to save, He will intervene when we call out for help – it's a sure thing. Our hope is founded on certainty.

Faith & Hope in working Partnership

An example of hope and faith in action: We had a visiting Pastor at our church when my eldest son was about eight years old. He told us the story of the miracle intervention of God to save. The Pastor recalled the day when some church brothers were travelling along the freeway in Melbourne. It was one of those freeways that are raised, with one roadway above another and crisscrossing here and there. Then suddenly a large semitrailer truck rammed through the railing of an upper roadway and careered directly towards this group of young Christian men in their car. They were sitting ducks and had nowhere to swerve out of its way. Then suddenly one of the young men screamed out, "*Jesus, save us!!!*" At that moment the truck lifted up and changed its trajectory and went over the car, crashing on the roadway behind them, leaving them completely unharmed. When my son heard this, he was wide-eyed and amazed. Jesus would actually do that if you were in danger!

Fast forward a couple of months and I was pregnant with my daughter, Amelia, but still lecturing at the local university. I had parked in the top carpark near the engineering building. (Now to give you some context, this carpark was the closest to the top of Mt Helen summit at the time, and was furthest from the main Ballarat-Geelong Road. It was not sealed but had a blue metal covering. Further down the hill was another carpark which was also not sealed and was basically gravelled. Below that carpark near its entrance from the roadway, was a large concrete culvert that was about 15 ft high and wide – not sure if it was for storm water or merely a creek, or perhaps both. To access the top car park, you entered the gravel carpark, then with the culvert to your right, turned left up the hill to the top car park and turned right into it.)

This particular day I had finished lectures and lesson preparations and jumped into the car to head home. It was an automatic car but something went seriously wrong. I turned on the key, put the car into reverse, and hardly began to put any pressure on the accelerator when the car went into sudden turbo mode at full speed. I immediately hit the brake (thankfully I hadn't moved more than a couple of feet at most) and did no longer had my foot on the accelerator, but the car engine was revving hard and the wheels were spinning at top speed, and throwing blue metal vigorously behind them. After a short time, the engine ceased to operate in what seemed like overdrive mode and went back to normal, but I was totally shocked and nervous about driving it home. Thankfully, the drive home was without incident.

Later when I arrived home, I told my husband about it but he brushed it off saying I must have had my foot on the accelerator. However, when driving an automatic, one foot stays on the floor whilst the other operates the brake and accelerator. Therefore, you cannot be doing braking and accelerating at the same time, which means I definitely had my foot on the brake – not the accelerator. Hearing this, he merely said, "*Well why didn't you just turn the key to the off position?*" Fair enough question /comment, but it all happened so quickly, that that thought didn't even register.

So, even though this had happened and I had explained everything truthfully and accurately, my husband assumed I was exaggerating, hallucinating or fabricating the whole story. That is until he travelled out to the university for some other reason, and this time had Nathan (my eldest son) in the car with him. He too parked in the top carpark near the engineering building. As they were leaving, my husband had just pulled out of the parking space and turned passed the cars towards the upper carpark exit, when the engine abruptly went into supercharge mode again and took off down the hill to the gravel carpark at top speed and headed straight for the culvert.

As the car began to run off road through the small amount of scrub towards the culvert, my son Nathan yelled out, "*Jesus, save us!*" and the car suddenly stopped. By this stage, the car was perhaps 1-1.5 metres from the edge and already on the incline.

I went back with Andrew to look at the scene the following day, and the skid marks were still very visible in the soft scrub floor. I even took a picture. The car had stopped directly in front of a sapling that was no taller than me and whose trunk was no thicker than about 2cm in diameter. The car was undamaged. No one was hurt. I am convinced that God heard Nathan's prayer and answered to save them.

Now was that *faith* or *hope* in operation? Both! Nathan heard the word and he had a firm **hope** that God would save him in a dangerous situation. Then whilst the incident was occurring, he held **faith** that God would do as He promised He'd do, so he prayed and God met his faith and saved them. God was, and still is, and ever will be, completely faithful to those who have placed their hope firmly in Him!

This example should highlight to you the importance of sharing testimonies of the miracles of God, as they speak of God's goodness, and give us hope (100% certainty) that when we face similar circumstances, our faith is grounded in Him.

Our Anchor

God's faithfulness should encourage perseverance in our confession of the things hoped for, no matter what the circumstances. We should not become lax in our hope because we have full assurance that His promises will be fulfilled. This same point is made by the author of Hebrews.

> "*And we desire that each one of you show the same diligence to the* ***full assurance of hope*** *until the end, that you do not become sluggish, but imitate those who through faith and patience inherit the promises.*" - **Hebrews 6:11-12 NKJV**

Then he continues by affirming that God does not lie and finally concludes:

> "[17]*Thus God, determining to show more abundantly to the heirs of promise the immutability of His counsel, confirmed it by an oath,* [18]*that by two immutable things, in which it is impossible for God to lie, we might have strong consolation, who have fled for refuge to lay hold of the* ***hope*** *set before us.* [19]*This* ***hope*** *we have as an* ***anchor*** *of the soul, both sure and steadfast, and which enters the Presence behind the veil,* [20]*where the forerunner has entered for us, even Jesus, having become High Priest forever according to the order of Melchizedek.*" – **Hebrews 6:17-20 NKJV**

God's promise was made sure by the addition of an oath.

However, the solidness of God's steadfast and reliable word is shored up even more because our hope has entered behind the veil, where Jesus has gone as a forerunner on our behalf, and is making intercession for us before the Father.

Thus, we in the New Testament have greater reason to hope, for not only is God's character beyond reproach and His promises absolutely certain, but Jesus has become our great high priest on our behalf.

What is the object of our hope? Paul states in Titus 1:1-2 that we have hope of eternal life that God promised.

> "[1]*Paul, a bondservant of God and an apostle of Jesus Christ, according to the faith of God's elect and the acknowledgment of the truth which accords with godliness,* [2]***in hope of eternal life*** *which God, who cannot lie, promised before time began,*" – **Titus 1:1-2 NKJV**

Eternal life is our future possession, and thus, an object of hope. God has prepared it all for us. It's there waiting and therefore, we stay the course laid in for us and rest our hope in Him. His blood and sacrifice opened the door to Heaven and life in eternity for us. Christ, Himself, is the grounds of our hope. Now Jesus is our Hope of Glory.

> "*To them God willed to make known what are the riches of the glory of this mystery among the Gentiles: which is Christ in you, the hope of glory.*" – **Colossians 1:27 NKJV**

Again, in another opening remark, Paul greets Timothy, and calls Jesus Christ, our hope,

> "*Paul, an apostle of Jesus Christ, by the commandment of God our Savior and the* ***Lord Jesus Christ, our***

hope" – 1Timothy 1:1 - NKJV

Further to that, our hope is that when Christ returns, the divine saving work will be brought to a head, and we will all be caught up with Him into paradise. We are not like those who have no hope. Paul tells this to the Thessalonians:

> "[13]*But I do not want you to be ignorant, brethren, concerning those who have fallen asleep, lest you sorrow as others who have no hope.* [14]*For if we believe that Jesus died and rose again, even so God will bring with Him those who sleep in Jesus.*
>
> [15]*For this we say to you by the word of the Lord, that we who are alive and remain until the coming of the Lord will by no means precede those who are asleep.* [16]*For the Lord Himself will descend from heaven with a shout, with the voice of an archangel, and with the trumpet of God. And the dead in Christ will rise first.* [17]*Then we who are alive and remain shall be caught up together with them in the clouds to meet the Lord in the air. And thus, we shall always be with the Lord.*" – **1 Thessalonians 4:13-17 - NKJV**

We now have a living hope through Jesus' death and resurrection.

> "[3]*Blessed be the God and Father of our Lord Jesus Christ, who according to His abundant mercy has begotten us again to a* ***living hope*** *through the resurrection of Jesus Christ from the dead,* [4] *to an inheritance incorruptible and undefiled and that does not fade away, reserved in heaven for you*" – **1Peter 1:3-4 NKJV**

It's not a dead or vain hope, but living and vibrant. It spurs us on and is cause for us to forge ahead despite any difficulties we are facing. The promise is sealed in His Word:

> "*For as in Adam all die, even so in Christ all shall be made alive.*" – **1 Corinthians 15:22 NKJV**

We do not perish once we die. Christ is the first fruits of the dead.

> "*But now Christ is risen from the dead, and has become the first-fruits of those who have fallen asleep.*" – **1 Corinthians 15:20 NKJV**

Our Guarantee

Christ is the proof and now because of His saving grace and because it is no longer I that live but Christ in me, the hope of resurrection is made sure. In fact, our inheritance has been further guaranteed by the Holy Spirit!

> "[4]*For we who are in this tent groan, being burdened, not because we want to be unclothed, but further clothed, that mortality may be swallowed up by life.* [5]*Now He who has prepared us for this very thing is God, who also has given us the Spirit as a* ***guarantee.***" – **2 Corinthians 5:4-5 NKJV**

> "[13]*In Him you also trusted, after you heard the word of truth, the gospel of your salvation; in whom also, having believed, you were sealed with the Holy Spirit of promise,* [14]*who is the* ***guarantee of our inheritance*** *until the redemption of the purchased possession, to the praise of His glory.*" - **Ephesians 1:13-14 NKJV**

> "[20]*For all the promises of God in Him are Yes, and in Him Amen, to the glory of God through us.* [21]*Now He*

who establishes us with you in Christ and has anointed us is God, [22]who also has sealed us and given us the Spirit in our hearts as a ***guarantee****."* - **2 Corinthians 1:20-22 – NKJV**

Finally, Paul confidently quotes Isaiah 64:4 as our hope,

> "*But as it is written: 'Eye has not seen, nor ear heard, nor have entered into the heart of man, the things which God has prepared for those who love Him.'*" – **1 Corinthians 2:9 NKJV**

Chapter 5

The Intimacy Factor

~~~~~~~~~~~~~~

In Chapter One I mentioned that praise and worship in the midst of turmoil demonstrates to God our trust and faith in Him, and it pleases Him greatly. Worship and intimacy in prayer takes our eyes off the situation and places it squarely back on Jesus. At this time the problems melt into insignificance in the light of who He is. It is from that position that our faith grows – i.e. as we look and behold Him.

Love and adoration are the foundation of faith. Without love, without drawing close in relationship to truly know the Master of all things, how can we have the kind of faith that knows, that it knows, and is unshakably certain? Belief in your head is not the same as knowledge in your heart. So, what is it to truly love God with all our heart, mind, soul, and strength? (Deuteronomy 6:5; 11:13; 13:3; and 30:6) (See also Matthew 22:37; Mark 12:30; and Luke 10:27 in which Jesus answered a lawyer who had inquired which was the greatest command.) How can we love someone we cannot see, let alone have faith in Him?

Faith, Hope & Love

In speaking to the church in Corinth (1 Corinthians 12), Paul emphasises the fact that even though we have different gifts and abilities, God does not see one as better than the others but that we are all important and of equal value in his eyes. Together we make up Christ's body, all members functioning together for the benefit of the whole. As such, it is God who appoints ministries and provides gifts to each
~~~~~~~~~~~~~~

as He sees fit to achieve the body's optimum functionality.

Paul ends this discourse by adding in verse 31,

> "*But earnestly desire the best gifts. And yet I show you a more excellent way.*" – **1 Corinthians 12:31 NKJV**

In the following chapter he talks about the most important characteristic of a Christian – not how many gifts he has, but how much he ***loves***.

Then as the chapter concludes he reminds the Corinthians that all the gifts are completely unnecessary in Paradise because everything will be made clear to us. However,

> "*Now these three remain: faith, hope and love. But the greatest of these is love.*" – **1 Corinthians 13:13 NIV**

In other words, the gifts may "pass away" but these attributes, (i.e. faith, hope and love), will always be required in Heaven. Why is this? He explains that the gifts are there for the work of the Kingdom and to ultimately bring glory to God, not the person using them.

(I like to think of them as a Spiritual box of tools. When someone is given a box of tools, it doesn't make him suddenly a master builder, nor even a better person. Likewise, when we are given the gifts, as wonderful as these gifts are, and as privileged that we are to be able to use them through the power of God's Holy Spirit, they remain tools for Christ to use through us. They do not make us suddenly better Christians, nor do they upgrade our status or prestige in the realm of Christendom. I believe Paul makes this point.

Further, they are not dependent on our holiness but God's generosity, and once given are irrevocable. In other words, no matter the spiritual and love climate of one's heart, they remain. God does not take them back and this is why Jesus tells us in Matthew 7:22-23 that many will complain to Him when they are locked out of heaven, that they were out prophesying, casting out demons and do many wonders all in His name. What is Jesus' response? "*I never knew you; depart from Me, you who practice lawlessness.*"

Thus, it is possible to use the gifts merely to bolster up you own image/ministry, or to do your own thing without reference to God. Jesus calls this practicing lawlessness. The kind of people He will take to Himself in His Kingdom will be those who know and love Him enough to work with Him, follow His lead and instructions, and who have no other ulterior motive beyond their great love for Him.)

Add to all this, that the gifts will no longer be useful in heaven. We will have everything we need: all knowledge, all wisdom, and we'll no longer need healings, or miracles etc. Everything is provided in God's heavenly house. There is nothing evil there. Therefore, the gifts, that were essential for the work of God on earth, will "pass away" once we cross heaven's threshold. Subsequently, being able to use the gifts does not qualify anyone for an eternity where they (the gifts) are no longer required!

So, why are faith, hope and love the attributes of the heart that will forever remain? Paul explained that without love, we are nothing, and what we do adds up to nothing, even if we sacrifice our lives for others. In fact, in Deuteronomy 6:5, the Israelites were commanded to love God above everything, and then to love others:

> "*You shall love the LORD your God with all your heart, with all your soul, and with all your strength.*" – **Deuteronomy 6:5 NKJV**

And

> *"... you shall love your neighbour as yourself"* – **Leviticus 19:18b NKJV**

Jesus reiterates this when responding to the lawyer's question about the **greatest commandment**.

> *"Jesus said to him, "'You shall love the LORD your God with all your heart, with all your soul, and with all your mind.' "This is the first and great commandment, and the second is like it: 'You shall love your neighbour as yourself.' On these two commandments hang all the Law and the Prophets."* – **Matthew 22:37-40 NKJV**

(Similar passages are found in Mark 12:30-31 and in Luke 10:27) Jesus also told His disciples (in John's gospel) that a He was also giving to them new commandment.

> *"A new commandment I give to you, that you love one another; as I have loved you, that you also love one another."* - **John 13:34 NKJV**

Loving others as oneself was no longer sufficient. How many people truly love themselves? Now we are to love in a similar fashion to the way Jesus demonstrated His love to the disciples, and to others – that is, totally unconditionally!! Love is the most important Christian attribute, and how we behave (i.e. doing the will of God as well as good works) will demonstrate how much we love. It's the proof of love.

So how does this relate to faith and hope? In the preceding chapters I have already explained these connections, but in case it was not clear, if you do not have a close relationship with God in love, how can you truly know Him? As in any relationship, it takes time to know a person completely. Yes, your study of the Bible can help facilitate this, but just reading a book about someone, does not mean we know all the intimate details about them. Head knowledge is not heart knowledge. That comes as we develop our relationship with that person.

Likewise, our relationship not only depends on our study of the word, but on the time we spend with Jesus, Himself. It is then that the word becomes alive to us giving us understanding of the mysteries He has hidden there for us to find. Most importantly, however, we begin to know His heart both towards us and for mankind. Over time, our experiences with God, through our struggles and times of need, reinforce our trust and absolute ***faith*** in God. Further, we also develop a solid ***hope*** that this kind of love, friendship, and support will continue into the future, and into eternity. Only in love can hope and faith be built. Love is the foundation upon which the faith and hope rest. Therefore, love and intimacy are essential for faith and hope to exist, and the reason why Paul describes it as the greatest and better way.

Who am I in God's Eyes?

As I briefly mentioned previously, one of the greatest weapons the enemy uses against us constantly, is to make us doubt God's love for us. To put it another way, knowing you love God is one thing, but knowing you are loved by God is quite another. How often have we thought, "*Yeah, I know God can do it, but will He actually do it for me? Afterall, I'm a terrible Christian.*" Obviously, this is a doubt from the enemy, but since this tactic is obvious, why does the enemy continue to use it? Because the enemy knows that if we're convinced that we're not worthy and not loved, we will not have faith in God to see manifest the things for which we have prayed. A bad self-image means little to no faith, and similarly for our Christian hope.

It has been said that it is only through our perception of God that we are the people we are. If we see God as judgemental, we will be judgemental. If we see God as good, we will see that we are also born to be good. The Bible agrees with this. Paul states that as we behold Him, we are changed into His image. (2 Corinthians 3:18) Unfortunately, most of us view Father God as similar to our own earthly father, and if that was a negative experience, it will have tainted the way we view our heavenly Father. What is needed in this case, is a correct and truthful perspective of Father God, and this can only take place as we renew our minds. These two things (i.e. how we see God and thus, how we see ourselves) are imperative.

Consider Gideon: When the angel visited him, he extolled the virtues of Gideon, even though he was weak and hiding. Instead of rejoicing that God had these thoughts about him and wanted to use him for His (God's) glory, Gideon complained! How could he possibly be strong when God had forsaken him, (and Israel for that matter), and besides, his personal status was so low that he was a no body. No one would listen to him let alone fight for him!

Gideon was as good as his self-image even though the angel told him who he really was at that point in time. However, we know despite that, he proceeded to do the will of God, albeit reluctantly at first and at night in case there was any opposition. By the end of the story though, God had enabled Gideon to fulfil the promise of rescuing the nation.

Often times, tragedy can bring offence to our lives and this then leads to unbelief as we build a doctrine on our circumstances (as in Gideon's case), instead of believing God for who He actually is. How important then, it is to have a true self-image, not scarred because of personal tragedies, and not over inflated because of the way we have been promoted.

How then can we overcome this seemingly insurmountable hurdle of poor or incorrect self-image? Firstly, the word states,

> "*My people are destroyed for* ***lack of knowledge.***" – **Hosea 4:6 NKJV**

As mentioned, this knowledge comes through 1) the word of God and 2) our relationship with Father God.

As we study the word and become familiar with the Word, we realise what God thinks about us, and because of His great love, how valuable we are to Him. So valuable in fact, that He sent Jesus to die in our place.

> "*For God so loved the world that He gave His only begotten Son, that whoever believes in Him should not perish but have everlasting life.*" – **John 3:16 NKJV**

Out of all the disciples, John calls himself "the one whom Jesus loved". His self-image was based on how much God loved him, not on what he accomplished.

In Psalm 91 it says,

> "'*Because he has set his love upon Me, therefore I will deliver him; I will set him on high, because he has known My name. He shall call upon Me, and I will answer him; I will be with him in trouble; I will deliver him and honour him. With long life I will satisfy him, and show him My salvation.*'" – **Psalm 91:14-16 NKJV**

John understood the love of God and as a result, John set his love on Him.

> "*We love Him because He first loved us.*" – **1 John 4:19 NKJV**

In accordance with the promise in Psalm 91 quoted above, John was also "*satisfied with long life*", and even though tradition tells that Rome tried to kill him several times, they failed in their attempts, having to exile him to the Island of Patmos instead. Yet even there, John was still mightily used by God. (His dreams and visions became the Book of Revelation in the New Testament.) So, why was he satisfied with long life? Because he set his love upon God. It is difficult to love God if you don't believe you are loved by God, but John knew God intimately, and made it clear that loving God in return was the biggest requirement of any Christian believer.

When Jesus was baptised in the Jordan by John the Baptiser, the Father publicly declared that Jesus was His Son in whom He was well pleased. This is a huge affirmation of love. It has been said that when a Jewish boy underwent his bar mitzvah, it was the tradition for the father to put his son on his shoulders and declare publicly how proud he was of his son. Joseph, not being Jesus' true father, but rather his adoptive parent, was unlikely to have done this. However, Father God made up for any lack of this worldly affirmation by doing this at Jesus' baptism.

If it was so important for Father God to ensure He affirmed His love for Jesus, how much more is it important that we know and understand that we too, as His children, are so very loved? In the book of Jeremiah, we learn that God knows us from the time He formed us in our mother's womb.

"Before I formed you in the womb, I knew you" – **Jeremiah 1:5a NKJV**

He not only knows us but loved us before we could love Him back, or do anything to please Him. Dr Brian Simmons, author of the Passion Translation, and weekly devotional on the PassionAndFire.com website, wrote the following word from the Spirit of God,

> *"How greatly I look forward to that journey of discovery with you, My child! You see, I well know the plans I have for you. I imagined you within My heart before time began. I planned and formed you, and oh, how I delight in you. Step into My embrace today and enjoy My delight.*
>
> *I don't want you striving and straining to conform to what this world says is good and valuable. I want you at rest in My love. Come rest in My heart and drink in My pleasure, for I am rejoicing over you — even now. Yes, it's true. I am not waiting for you to change or grow before I enjoy you. Your value doesn't increase with time; I cherish you at every stage of your growth.*
>
> *Receive this truth today: I couldn't love you any more than I already do. I love you completely, thoroughly, and eternally, just the way you are. Now, love yourself, too, and embrace your true identity in Me so that you are free to shine and stand out. I am changing you from one brighter level of glory to another into the image of My Son, and through you, the world will see who I truly am."*[9]

Knowing how much we are loved by God inspires us to

---

9 Brian Simmons, "*Passion and Fire*" weekly devotional series, May 8th 2025

draw close and love Him even more. We love Him because He first loved us!

Secondly, we also need to know Him more intimately, so close, in fact, that we can see our reflection in His eyes, for only in this manner can we be truly changed. That sounds poetic, but Paul says in 2 Corinthians 3:18

> "*But we all, with unveiled face, beholding as in a mirror the glory of the Lord, are being transformed into the same image from glory to glory, just as by the Spirit of the Lord.*" – **2 Corinthians 3:18 NKJV**

Being able to see Him, and therefore, ourselves, should encourage us, because it enables us to see how much we have already grown in Him, and to further transform us from glory to greater glory until we even look like Him. As we begin to look more and more like Him, we also understand and love Him all the more. This strengthens our confidence in Him, which is in turn, both faith building and hope sustaining.

OK, I get it! How do we look at God? We are in the flesh, and He is in the Spirit! How can the physical possibly "see" things in the Spirit realm? Do we all need to be prophetic? That would be grand, but we see Him in the Word of God and through our relationship experience with Him.

It's not enough to simply read or approach the word of God like any other book. It requires that we meditate upon it, to spend time pondering the deeper truths it contains, and studying it with the aid of the Holy Spirit who reveals its greater mysteries.

However, simply knowing *about* Him is not enough to be able to see and recognise Him. We need the knowledge of the truth of His Word cemented in our spirits through our experience with Him. That is, we need to know Him fully, not just about Him! Sure, we can know aspects of him throughout life's ups and downs, but the only real way to gain that full knowledge of Him, is through deliberate quiet time with Him, just to listen to Him, to be real before Him, and to pray humbly. It is in these quiet times with Him that we begin to really see and experience with our spirit man, the real Jesus now living in us. We see and hear His heart for us and for the lost. This kind of deep knowing the Bible calls "*epignosis*"[10] (Greek word meaning to know fully - see footnote).

The unusual thing is that the more we spend time with Him, the more we desire to spend time with Him. It seems upside down, and back to front somehow. (It's like saying that the more we eat, the hungrier we get.) Conversely, the less time we spend with Him, the less time we want to spend with Him. Subsequently, if we brush aside this special time with Him for "more interesting" things, (e.g. for our phones, or games, or church activities, or preparation for sermons & worship services, or just the business of life), the less we will desire Him, and the easier it is for us to be deceived and distracted by the enemy. It is so much easier for the enemy to sow doubt during these times. Instead of countering the enemy's barrage of lies with our daily input of truth, we listen to the lies, meditate upon them, and believe them. This then becomes the gateway for not only compromised values and sin to dictate how we should behave, but for shame, despondency, dis

---

10 "*The term "epignosis" refers to a deep, thorough, and precise knowledge. It implies a full understanding or discernment that goes beyond mere factual awareness. In the New Testament, it often denotes a spiritual or moral insight that is granted by God, particularly in the context of knowing Christ and His will*" - retrieved from https://biblehub.com/greek/1922.htm. Strongs #1922

appointment, low self-esteem and even regret, (to name afew) to speak into our lives instead.
This is why Paul prays for our knowledge of Him to increase, praying:

> "*that the God of our Lord Jesus Christ, the Father of glory, may give to you the spirit of* ***wisdom and revelation in the knowledge of Him****, the eyes of your understanding being enlightened; that you may* ***know*** *what is the hope of His calling, what are the riches of the glory of His inheritance in the saints, and what is the exceeding greatness of His power* ***toward us who believe****, according to the working of His mighty power which He worked in Christ when He raised Him from the dead and seated Him at His right hand in the heavenly places, far above all principality and power and might and dominion, and every name that is named, not only in this age but also in that which is to come. And He put all things under His feet, and gave Him to be head over all things to the church, which is His body, the fullness of Him who fills all in all.*" – **Ephesians 1:16-23 NKJV**

The Word and our intimate time with Him, complement each other so well. They work hand in hand. When our knowledge of Him expands through both the logos and the rhema Word of God, we understand more of His love and His goodness towards us, and how He desires us to draw close in love. We are so valuable to Him.

God's Blood Covenant with Us

To help you understand how much you are loved, I really need to talk about God's covenant to us. God so loved the world that He gave Jesus. Through Jesus' death and resurrection not only was the debt of our sins paid, but Jesus stripped our sin nature and its sinful motivations (our old man) from us, but He also made a New Covenant on our behalf to enable us to live a Godly life. That's how much He loves us and how valuable we are in His sight.

Covenants, or more accurately "blood covenants", were rituals from ancient times. In fact, some have speculated that because blood covenants are still practiced by every isolated primitive people in the world, it is evidence of a single ancient origin when people all lived in close proximity. You might be interested in reading about Stanley's travels in Africa[11], and how the tribes he encountered were already very fluent in cutting covenants - covenants about which he knew nothing. There is also ancient archaeological evidence from other countries such as India, China, Borneo and other island countries, that blood covenants existed well before western man could have introduced them. In fact, western man has largely forgotten about them. So, the origin could have easily been with God. Perhaps He discussed this with Adam or even Noah. We may never know.

A blood covenant was usually cut for one of three reasons:

> 1) It was made between two tribes when one was a lot stronger than the other, and the weaker did not want to be destroyed.
>
> 2) Two people doing similar trade or business cut the covenant so that neither would take advantage of the other.
>
> 3) If two people were devoted to each other. Example: David and Jonathon.

---

11 *The Blood Covenant* by E. W. Kenyon, (c) Copyright 2016, Crossreach Publications

The terms of the covenant depended on the situation of course, and were generally forged for the benefit to both parties.

* In order for the covenant to be cut, the chiefs or representatives from both parties stood before a priest or some officiate, usually in some public setting.

* They exchanged gifts to show that, should the person require it, all the belongings of the giving party are now at the disposal of the receiver. This did not mean that this privilege could be abused, but that if circumstances absolutely required it, the blood brothers would stand together, combining resources, fighting skills or whatever, to see the situation through to its conclusion.

* Then the priest poured a cup of wine, and after making an incision in the arm or hand of both people, allowed the blood from each to drip into the wine. Both parties then drank this blood-wine mixture.

* After this, the two parties would seal the deal by placing their wounds together in order to mingle the blood. Alternatively, they would lick each other's wounds. This mingling is symbolic that the two have become blood brothers - that is, closer than real brothers. If you were to look at one party it was understood that it was the same as looking at the other, and they must be treated as such.

* Covenants could not be broken under ***any*** circumstances. If someone was to break a covenant, he was not only cursed, but deserved death. It was also ex-

pected that these covenants were kept and revered by the children to the third and fourth generation. A covenant was/is perpetual, indissoluble and simply could not/cannot be annulled.

> * After the ceremony, memorial trees were planted, or if this was not possible, a monument of stones was erected. If neither memorial could be employed, some other memorial was agreed upon. These were to remind the descendants who follow, of the covenant that was made, and that they too are partners in this unbreakable covenant.

We can see this play out between God and Abraham. Abraham was told to journey to a place God would show and give him, and God would multiply him greatly. Then a little later in Genesis, we see this covenant is solemnised when Abraham is asked by God to get some animals to be His "stand in" or representative, and to cut them in half to shed the blood for Him. God then appears as a fiery pot walking between them. (See Genesis 15 & 17) Conversely, Abraham's blood shedding was the through the process of circumcision, which also became the memorial for successive generations.

> "*And My covenant shall be in your flesh for an everlasting Covenant.*" – **Genesis 17:13 NKJV**

Both God and Abraham knew exactly the seriousness of ceremony, and what this would mean for Abraham's descendants. In fact, so solemn was the covenant that God said He wouldn't hide anything He was about to do from Abraham! (Genesis 18:17) And not only that, but Abraham was able to change God's mind about how many righteous people would prevent the destruction of the cities. God was true to His covenant with Abraham.

Nevertheless, God wanted to be sure that Abraham would live up to his side of the covenant and asked Abraham to offer up his son to Him. Abraham knew that because of the terms of the covenant, God *had* to keep His promise to birth nations through Isaac, (Genesis 17:19) so, he reasoned that God would raise him from the dead again even though He'd asked Abraham to sacrifice him. Such was the power of covenant!

{Just a side note here: Abraham did not always get it right. He was human afterall. For example, Abraham told Pharoah that Sarah was his sister (she was actually his half sister, so it wasn't exactly false), but he neglected to reveal that she was also his wife. This omission almost had Sarah taken into Pharoah's bed chamber until God intervened! Then later, he and Sarah had Ishmael when they attempted to fulfil the promise in their own strength.

However, in the fullness of time, God proved Himself true to His promises when Sarah birthed Isaac. Abraham had seen, first hand, the power of God at work when God sent fire and brimstone against Sodom and Gomorrah. Now Abraham also witnessed how God had kept His promise, even though it was impossible, in human terms, for Sarah give birth in her old age. God could do all this; therefore, Abraham's faith was now sufficient for him to believe and trust that God could also raise Isaac from the dead, and keep the covenant God had made with him.}

When the Israelites were enslaved in Egypt, God delivered them because He heard their cries and He remembered His same covenant to them. By this time, they had become a nation, so God gave Moses laws for them to live by, and cut a new covenant – the terms of which are given in Exodus 22. The sprinkling of blood then sealed this. All those present knew what this meant. The covenant was not to be broken, or there would be a huge penalty – curses and death, but so long as they kept covenant, God would bless them. Note: It wasn't a replacement for the Abrahamic covenant, but an outcome or reason for the Mosaic covenant. He was giving them a code to live by that would be beneficial to them, so that He could continue to bless Abraham's seed.

OK, how does all this relate to the ***New Covenant*** and therefore, to us? When Jesus announced at the Passover Supper that the wine they were about to drink was the blood of the New Covenant, His statement no doubt, shocked the disciples. One moment they are celebrating the Passover Lamb, and recalling how God kept covenant with Israel. In the next moment Jesus was talking about a whole new covenant, where He was to be the new Spotless Lamb that caused the penalty of sin to pass over men without executing judgement. The whole Jewish culture revolved around the Mosaic Covenant. Now Jesus was replacing thousands of years of that culture. They knew as they drunk that wine, they were entering into a binding agreement.

To see better how this works, let's now do a comparison between the bullets points above that describe how a blood covenant is cut, and the New Covenant that Christ cut for us:

1) When Jesus suffered and died, it was His blood as both man and God that sealed the covenant. (The circumcision of the New Covenant was of man's heart.) Jesus was also the high priest that presented that offering to the Holy of Holies in the temple of God in Heaven. (Remember how He told Mary not to touch Him because He needed to first ascend to the Father as the pure and spotless One.) This was to completely fulfil all the terms of the Mosaic

Covenant/Law and usher in the terms of the New.

Jesus is now the great High Priest who ministers in the true Tabernacle not one built with hands, and who now makes intercession for us. He is our true mediator between us and God. We are no longer under any condemnation. We stand completely justified. He is now our righteousness.

2) In exchange for all that we are, we now have complete access to everything that He has. Peter says that:

> "*His divine power has given to us all things that pertain to life and godliness, through the knowledge of Him who called us by glory and virtue, by which have been given to us exceedingly great and precious promises, that through these you may be partakers of the divine nature*" - **2 Peter 1:3-4 NKJV**

He has also given us the Holy Spirit as a Guide, Counsellor and Comforter, and enabled us to use His Spiritual gifts. He has withheld nothing from us. Paul even describes us as spiritual heirs of Abraham and therefore, we have access to the blessings of the Abrahamic Covenant as well.

> "*Therefore, know that only those who are of faith are sons of Abraham. And the Scripture, foreseeing that God would justify the Gentiles by faith, preached the gospel to Abraham beforehand, saying, 'In you all the nations shall be blessed" So then those who are of faith are blessed with believing Abraham.*' - **Galatians 3:7-9 NKJV**

3) Jesus, our great high priest, taking the cup representing His blood, blessed it before God the Father and in front of His disciples, and drank it with them as representative of both God and man, thus sealing the deal - the New Covenant was now cut on our behalf, and would be fulfilled by His death!

4) Further, now He is closer than any earthly brother. We have become partakers of the Divine Nature. Paul says that it is no longer I who live but Christ who lives in me (Gal 2:20). It doesn't get any closer. God the Father looks at us and sees Jesus. I am in Him and He is in me. Because of this, we have authority and power in His Name, and wherever the enemy sees us, he sees Jesus and therefore, the enemy knows that he is under authority. The other benefit is that God who, as the stronger party joined to us, has covenanted to protect us.

5) The covenant is a very solemn legal agreement. None of this is dependent on how you merely feel. We have been united with Christ as a new man *joined to God, Himself.* God takes that very seriously. It doesn't disappear if you wake up feeling grumpy or a complete failure. We are legally under the New Covenant, and it is eternal.

6) And what was the memorial Jesus gave to us? As He took the cup He said, "*As often as you do these things, do them in remembrance of Me!*" This was an everlasting covenant, with a memorial that we re-enact every time we have communion!

I hope you are following to this point. The enormity of this transaction can literally cause you sit back and exclaim, "*Wow!*" It's so incredible that it poses the question: why would God go to the trouble to create a blood covenant and then to bind Himself to *man*? Surely, we could simply exist in a loving relationship without this union? John gives us a clue to that answer.

> "*This is the message which we have heard from Him*

and declare to you, that God is light and in Him is no darkness at all." – **1 John 1:5 NKJV**

It was/is not sufficient that we are merely forgiven. The motivation to sin had to be dealt with, or sin would continue. As the Bible clearly demonstrates, man is not capable of being sinless of himself. Of ourselves, we fail, and constantly *fall into darkness*. However, God yearns to have fellowship with us. John 3:16 stresses that God ***so*** loved that He gave. His whole purpose in creating us was to have eternal fellowship with us and share in His immense love. So, there is a problem. God is pure pristine light and light can have no fellowship with darkness.

"*What fellowship has righteousness with lawlessness? And what communion has light with darkness?*" – **2 Corinthians 6:14 NKJV**

Clearly, it was necessary not to just give us a new heart with new desires, but to be transformed also into *children of light*. This transformation into a new creation man not only changed our carnal desires, but as the Bride of Christ, it was essential to be wed to the King of kings and Lord of lords. There is no inter-species union here. We have been made totally compatible. We are spiritual beings of light. We now have the Father's Spiritual "DNA", and our hearts cry out, "*Abba! Father!*"

To illustrate this: if you can, imagine 4 cups. Three represent the Trinity and are each full to the brim with the same brilliant light. The 4th cup represents man. Man's cup is full of clear water. It is clear because of the blood of Jesus – the Pascal Lamb, has cleansed us of every sin. However, it contains water not light – water that can easily be dirtied up again. When Jesus forgave us our sins, He had to empty our sinful nature (represented by the water being poured out) and then fill us completely with Him – put the whole glass that represents Jesus, complete with light, into our empty one. Now we are like Him because as Paul states,

> "*I have been crucified with Christ; it is no longer I who live, but Christ lives in me; and the life which I now live in the flesh I live by faith in the Son of God, who loved me and gave Himself for me.*" – **Galatians 2:20 NKJV**

Not only that but Paul also states,

> "*For in Him dwells all the fullness of the Godhead bodily*" – **Colossians 2:9 NKJV,**

which means that both the Father and the Holy Spirit live in Jesus. So now place those glasses (the one representing the Father and the one representing the Holy Spirit) into the stack. Further, God has poured out His Spirit upon us so that now there is not just a spring or fountain (John 4:14) welling up from within, but now there are rivers of living water flowing out from us (John 7:38). So, if it were possible to have a jug full of light, you could pour this light out over the whole thing until it flowed out to the world.

Now we are completely compatible with God and are able to have fellowship with Him. God's desire was always to love and be loved by man. He loves not because man was innocent/naive and knew no better, not because there was a set of rules and Laws describing what can and cannot be done in order to please God, not because we work hard at the church or in charitable deeds, but it was the reason He created us.

What an astounding tale of God's pursuance of man's heart! What extraordinary love God has for us! Why would you want to choose anything else! He is more than we could ever want or need – greater than any selfish desire that sin could conjure.

Now we are seated with Christ in Heavenly places (Ephesians 2:6). We now have a glimpse of how He views and loves us, and how important we are to Him. Our perspective completely changes to see as He sees. Knowing who we are in Him increases our faith in Him that He will do for us the things He has promised. This in turn, solidifies our hope for a future with Him.

Further, greater is He that is in us than he who is in the world, (1 John 4:4). This means that we have authority over and are totally victorious over the enemy through Christ Jesus. Our self-image is so important to our faith, but is so often what is attacked by the enemy of our souls. However, we can overcome the tactics of the enemy when we know who we really are in Christ and how valued we are by Him.

What Does the Bible Say About Me?

That being said, here are just a few Scriptures references for you to look up and chew/meditate over. They were collected over the years, so were not all my findings. Some were from a handout given to me as a Bible College student, some were from Ps Liz Bailey from Victoria, Australia, and others from unknown sources in my past. I hope you find them encouraging as you read through them and allow the Holy Spirit to weld them to your heart. It may even help to write out the particular verses that resonate with you, and recite them out loud, (since faith comes from hearing the word of God). This will help build up your most holy faith. Here they are:

I Am Accepted in Christ:

* I am God's child - John 1:12

* I am loved unconditionally - John 3:16

* I am Christ's friend - John 15:15

* I am united with the Lord, and one with Him in spirit - 1 Corinthians 6:17

* 1 Corinthians 6:20 I have been bought with a price; I belong to God

* I am a member of Christ's body - 1 Corinthians 12:27

* I was set apart by God before I was born - Gal 1:15

* I am a saint - Ephesians 1:1

* I am blessed with all blessings - Ephesians 1:3

* I was chosen by God before He created the world - Ephesians 1:4

* I have been predestined to sonship - Ephesians 1:5

* I am accepted in the Beloved - Ephesians 1:6

* I am sealed with the promise of the Holy Spirit - Ephesians 1:13

* I am quickened together with Christ - Eph 2:5

* I have direct access to God through the Holy Spirit - Ephesians 2:18

* I am a member of God's household - Ephesians 2:19

* I am washed in His blood - Revelation 1:5

Who I Am in Christ

* I am forgiven - Colossians 1:14

* I am justified - Romans 5:18

* I am forever free from condemnation - Romans 8:1-2; 33-34

* I'm free from the power of sin - Romans 6:14a

* I'm free from the law of sin and death - Rom 8:2

* I'm free from the curse of the law - Galatians. 3:13

* I'm more than a conqueror - Romans 8:37; 1John 2:14; 4:4; 5:4

* I'm the righteousness of God in Christ - 2 Cor 5:21

* I'm created in righteousness and true holiness - Ephesians. 4:24

* I'm complete in Christ - Colossians 2:10

* I'm seated with Christ in heavenly places - Eph 2:6

* I'm a king and priest unto God - 1 Peter 2:5,9; Revelation 5:10

* I have the greater One dwelling in me - 1 John 4:4

* I can do anything in Christ - Philippians 4:13

* I am a joint-heir with Jesus - Romans 8:17; Ephesians 1:13, 14

* I am rich in the things of God - 2 Corinthians 8:9

* I'm competent in Christ - 2 Corinthians 3:4-5

* I have everything necessary for a life of godliness - 2 Peter 1:3

I Am Secure in Christ

* I can't get away from God - Psalms 139:6-10

* I am assured that all things work together for good Romans 8:28

* I cannot be separated from the love of God - Romans 8:35-39

* I have been established, anointed and sealed by God - 2 Corinthians 1:21

* Christ lives in me - Galatians 2:20

* I am confident that the good work God has begun in me will be perfected - Philippians 1:6

* I am a citizen of heaven - Philippians 3:20

* I am hidden with Christ in God - Colossians 3:3

* I have not been given a spirit of fear, but of power, love and a sound mind - 2 Timothy 1:7

* I can find grace and mercy in time of need - Hebrews 4:16

* I am born of God and the evil one cannot touch me - 1 John 5:18

I Am Significant in Christ

* My story is recorded in God's book - Psalms 139:16

* I am the salt and light of the earth - Matthew 5:13,14

* I am a branch of the true vine, a channel of His life - John 15:15

* I have been chosen and appointed to bear fruit - John 15:16

* I am a personal witness of Christ's - Acts 1:8

* I am more than a conqueror - Romans 8:37

* I am God's temple - 1 Corinthians 3:16

* I am victorious through Christ Jesus - 1 Cor 15:57

* I am a minister of reconciliation - 2 Cor 5:17-20

* I am God's co-worker - 2 Corinthians 6:1

* I am yoked together with other believers - 2 Corinthians 6:14

* I am to His praise - Ephesians 1:12

* I am unto His glory - Ephesians 1:14

* I am elevated to Heavenly places - Ephesians 2:6

* I am God's workmanship - Ephesians 2:10

* I can do all things through Christ who me - Philippians 4:13

* I am zealous for good works - Titus 2:14

* I am overcoming the world - 1 John 5:5

Once we understand just how much we are loved, and how valuable we are to the Father, our automatic response is to love Him in return. Because we love Him, we want to please Him and obey Him. It will be our automatic love response. If we know and love Him, we will not do anything to displease Him.

> "*Now by this we know that we know Him, if we keep His commandments. He who says, "I know Him," and does not keep His commandments, is a liar, and the truth is not in him.* ***But whoever keeps His word, truly the love of God is perfected in him****. By this we know that we are in Him. He who says he abides in Him ought himself also to walk just as He walked.*" – **1 John 2:3-6 NKJV**

This then is the test of our love for Him, and is a means of sustaining a holy and righteous life. When we love Him, we simply are not interested in doing anything which might be displeasing to Him.

This in turn, gives us confidence to approach the throne of grace where we can not only place our petitions before Him, but to worship and adore Him more. This is also the place where we can behold Him in all His glory and be further transformed. Such a beautiful process, and so lush with His love, mercy and grace towards us.

What Is It to Really Love God?

How can we be sure that we really love God? Is it just a feeling or something more? I believe the best description we have of love is found in Paul's first letter to the Corinthians chapter 13.

> "***Love*** *suffers long is kind; love does not envy;* ***love*** *does not parade itself, is not puffed up; does not behave rudely, does not seek its own, is not provoked, thinks no evil; does not rejoice in iniquity, but rejoices in the truth; bears all things, believes all things, hopes all things, endures all things.*" - **1 Corinthians 13:4-7 - NKJV**

I once heard someone suggest that if you can read that passage putting your own name wherever Paul has written, "love", it should be a good indicator of how much you really do love.

You might be thinking that this is talking about loving others only and not loving God. However, John states

> "*Beloved, let us love one another, for love is of God; and everyone who loves is born of God and knows God. He who does not love does not know God, for God is love.*"
>
> *"If someone says, "I love God," and hates his brother, he is a liar; for he who does not love his brother whom he has seen, how can he love God whom he has not seen? And this commandment we have from Him: that he who loves God must love his brother also.*" – **1 John 4:7-8, 20-21 NKJV**

Put simply, if we do not love others, we cannot argue that we love God? It's that black and white.

Conversely, we cannot love others if we do not love God. Our love and our idea of love is insufficient. We are commanded to love as He loved us – totally unconditionally. This is not our usual human response, but it is the divine response that we have access to through our love for Him. Loving others comes from the overflow of our love for God.

God has also demonstrated just what unconditional love looks like when He sent Jesus into the world for our sakes. We really have no excuse. If we love others like Jesus did, we must also be abiding in His love.

> "*If we love one another, God abides in us, and His love has been perfected in us...... God is love, and he who abides in love abides in God, and God in him.*" – **1 John 4:12, 16b NKJV**

In other words, loving others is a hallmark, a tale tail sign of our love for God, and that we belong to Him.

> "*By this all will know that you are My disciples, if you have love for one another.*" – **John 13:35 NKJV**

Love for others, particularly our brethren, is the proof of our love for God, but so is the amount of time we are prepared to give to Him daily, and how obedient we are to his commands. Jesus said,

> "*If you love Me, keep My commandments.*" – **John 14:15 NKJV**

Again in 1 John it says:

> "*If you keep My commandments, you will abide in My love, just as I have kept My Father's commandments and abide in His love.*" – **John 15:10 NKJV**

Love is more than a feeling. "Love has limbs" – that is, it is something that produces actions.

How can you test your love for God? Do you obey Him? Do you give Him priority throughout your day? Are you listening for the voice of your Beloved?

And how can you test your love of others in the church? Do you give them your time, or help them if they're in need? Do you make an effort to encourage them? Do you offer to help them move house, baby sit, invite them to dinner with you, or ask them out for a coffee after church, or even disciple/mentor the new believers? Do you visit the sick and/or the shut-ins? Do you offer to help with church setup, church cleaning, or some other form of serving? These are all indicators of how much you love. Love bears visible fruit!

As a Christian, when we can honestly say that we love others as He loves us, we can know that we love God, because He is love and His love empowers us to do so.

Moreover, this book is about faith. When we know someone well enough to love them fully and unconditionally, we can also trust them. This is the case with our relationship with God. When we know and love Him well, it's so much easier to know that we know, that He has everything in His hand. That is, to have faith in Him. We can trust Him to deliver on His promises and to answer our prayers according to His will, because He said He would!

Who Is Our God?

You may wish to use this list as a starting point for your own study. Search out the Scripture references associated with each of the descriptions given, and look for Scriptorial evidence of those statements that do not have references. By the time you finish, you will have an amazing picture of the greatness of our God!

* He is the Great "**I AM**", who was and is and who is to come. He always existed and will exist always. (Exodus 3:14; John 8:58)

* He is the **Alpha and the Omega** – the beginning and the end. (Revelation 1:8, 11; 21:6; 22:13)

* He is **infinite** and limitless (Psalm 90:2; Isaiah 40:28; Revelation 1:8; Hebrews 1:10; 2 Peter 3:8).

* He is **omnipotent** – all powerful, all mighty, who created all life and the entire universe, (Genesis 17:1; Isaiah 40:28; Jeremiah 32:17; Matthew 19:26; Hebrews 1:10).

* He is **omniscient** – all wise, all seeing and all knowing, (Psalm 147:5; Isaiah 40:28; 55:8-9; Romans 11:33).

* He is **omnipresent** – present in every place through all time, so that we can always find Him and be with Him, (Joshua 1:5; 1 Chronicles 16:34; Psalm 33:11; Hebrews 13:5).

* He rules absolutely, with all authority and reigns forever. His dominion has no end.

* He is independent – that is He self exists and is self-sufficient.

* He is immutable or unchanging – His character never changes nor needs to be changed.

* His purposes never change.

* He is perfect.

* He is incomparable.

* He is majestic and great above all things!

* He is glorious!

* He is Love, (1 John 4:8).

* His love is without end and without fluctuation.

* His love never fails.

* He is completely faithful (1Thessalonians 3:3; 1Timothy 2:13)

* He is the absolute Truth and can discern all truth. (John 14:6)

* His Word is Truth

* His Word never fails

* All His promises are true. They are "Yes!" and "Amen!" (2 Corinthians 1:20)

* He is righteous, and upright.

* He is Holy and Pure.

* He hates iniquity.

* He is just and loves justice.

* He has the power to execute judgment.

* He is a consuming fire.

* His mercy endures forever.

* He is gracious and gives grace freely to the humble, but He resists the proud. (Prov 3:34; James 4:6; 1 Peter 5:5)

* He is abundantly good and He is severe. (Romans 11:22)

* He forgives our iniquities. (Psalm 103:10; Isaiah 53:5)

* He saves us, not only for His glory but for His gladness.

* He is Light.

* He is the Way. (John 14:6)

* He is Life and the fountain of Life. (John 14:6; Psalm 36:9)

* He is generous

* He is a personal God who interacts with people individually.

* He identifies Himself with us.

* He longs for our fellowship

* He is Jealous for us.

* He knows everything about me.

* He does not make mistakes

* He believes in me.

* He is our comforter

* He is our righteousness.

* He is our provider

* He is our all sufficiency

* He is our shepherd

* He is our healer

* He is our banner

* He is our peace – the Prince of Peace

* He is the Lord of Hosts

* In Him is joy abundant

* He is kind

* He is admirable

* He is attractive

* He is praiseworthy

* He is the soon coming King

Old Testament Names of God:

Jehovah Nissi – The Lord my banner

Jehovah Rahh – The Lord my Shepherd

Jehovah Rapha – The Lord healer

Jehovah Shammah – The Lord is here

Jehovah Tsidkenu – The Lord our righteousness

Jehovah Jireh – The Lord will supply

Jehovah Sabaoth – The Lord of Hosts

Jehovah Shalom – The Lord is peace

Expressing Love Through Worship

Now, whilst it is true that faith without works is dead, it is equally true that works without love is merely dead religion. It is out of our love for God that we respond in obedience. We want to please our Beloved. If your friend asked you for help, you wouldn't think twice. You'd jump in and help. Likewise, God is more than just our beloved friend. We are His bride and He is our Husband. We want to please Him because of our great love for Him. In fact, Paul says in 1 Corinthians 13 that without love we are nothing, and also that our *works* equate to nothing without love. Therefore, the heart is very much involved.

So, if you are in a loving relationship with God and are waiting to see the manifestation of the prayers you have prayed in faith, the Bible specifically tells us to delight ourselves in the Lord.

> "*Delight yourself in the LORD, and He will give you the desires and petitions of your heart.*" – **Psalm 37:4 NKJV**

How can we delight ourselves in the Lord? - through our

quiet time with Him and through worship. Worship takes our eyes off the problem or need, and centres them back squarely upon God and His abilities, not our inadequacies to fix things, or provide things.

Worship also draws us into closer relationship with Him, because it demands more than just repetitive words and phrases. It demands our heart felt expression and devotion.

Consider the story of Cain and Abel. Here is an exert from my book "*Spirit Led Worship*", where I discuss this in depth:

It is unknown for certain whether God told Cain and Abel directly, or indirectly through Adam, that they should offer a sacrifice as means of saying thanks to God, or whether they thought it up themselves, but in Genesis chapter four the Bible say:

> "*In the course of time Cain brought to the Lord an offering of the fruit of the ground, and Abel also brought of the firstborn of his flock and of their fat portions. And the Lord had regard for Abel and his offering, but for Cain and his offering he had no regard. So, Cain was very angry, and his face fell.*" - **Genesis 4:2-5 ESV**

Cain was mentioned first as bringing his offering to the Lord. However, the verse gives the impression that both offerings may have been around the same time – we don't know, nor can we make assumptions. Did Cain think it up? Again, the fact is, we don't know.

What about his actual offering? Was something wrong with it? We don't know because the Bible does *not* say despite many teachers expressing their own personal point of view. All we do know is that it was *not acceptable* and Abel's was.

This *may* have been because of the actual offering itself (the type of offering) - although grain offerings were certainly acceptable in the Jewish Law, - or the quality may not have been up to scratch, but equally plausible, its unacceptable nature may have resulted from the *way* Cain offered it – either physically or in Cain's attitude!

Let's take a look at a few "Sacred Cows" very often discussed today. I do this not to somehow take a poke at anyone, or to indirectly negate someone else's teaching on offerings, but to scrutinize Cain and Abel's worship. If we are to worship in Spirit and in truth, we need to understand, as much as can be possible, what exactly was happening here. Why did God not accept Cain's offering, and are we in breach of doing the same?

Was the problem to do with first fruits or the lack thereof? Frankly, the Bible does not say. Therefore, we don't know for certain. We *do* know that the giving of first fruits was lawful. However, Cain and Abel lived approximately two thousand years before the law had even come into being. There was no written or stated law at that time! So, clearly, he was not breaking any religious laws.

Consider with me for a moment: If the government decided to change the side of the road the cars were to travel, and changed traffic laws accordingly overnight, and then made these laws retrospectively active for the past ten years, would it be fair to prosecute everyone who once travelled on the other side of the road. Of course not! But so often I hear this argument for why Cain's sacrifice was not acceptable. Clearly, they are not looking at what was really going on in Cain's heart.

That being said, there's probably no point to me arguing about the quality of Cain's offering as the Bible does not say either, so it would be speculation at best! Any discussions about Cain's crop in comparison to Abel's animal simply do not pan out logically, or have to include assumptions *not* found within the Scripture verses, in order to support such arguments. Yes, of course, we know that Abel's animal offering was the firstborn from his flock – it is stated – but to extrapolate that Abel's offering was accepted *because* his offering was the first fruit and Cain's was not, is to read meaning into the verse that is not there, nor supported by other Scriptures, all whilst ignoring all other possibilities.

Could the acceptability of Abel's offering lie in the fact that it was a *blood* offering and Cain's was not? Again, this falls under the Law of Moses and besides, grain offerings *were* acceptable thanksgiving offerings under the Law anyway. What then made Cain's sacrifice of worship unacceptable?

There is a couple of old sayings that parents often recite to their children when they are unhappy with the way a task is carried out. "*It's not what you do but how you do it!*" and "*It's not what you say but how you say it!*" The parent is essentially telling the child that their attitude, not their deed, needs a check. Perhaps it was Cain's heart attitude that was the real issue here.

Let's look at his attitude to see if perhaps that could have been an issue.

> "*So, Cain was very angry, and his face fell. [6]The Lord said to Cain, "Why are you angry, and why has your face fallen? [7]If you do well, will you not be accepted? And if you do not do well, sin is crouching at the door. Its desire is contrary to you, but you must rule over it." [8]Cain spoke to Abel his brother. And when they were in the field, Cain rose up against his brother Abel and*

killed him." - **Genesis 4:6-8 ESV**

Cain became angry (verse 5) that his sacrifice was not accepted. Now *if* his offering was substandard, and Cain knew so, he might have been a little annoyed at being caught out, or regretted his choice, but hardly angry – especially enough to murder his brother! Rather, a spirit of entitlement usually manifests when someone believes their effort is every bit as good as someone else's, and yet ignored or passed over. He would have worked quite hard tilling the soil, planting, and then keeping the wild animals away from the crop until it was ready. He obviously thought what he had to offer was just *as good as* his brother's, so why wasn't he also accepted?

God then addresses Cain about his offering. God has no favourites. If Cain does it right, he'll also be commended, but as it is, his new attitude and thoughts of unfairness towards his brother could lead to sin. Cain did not take heed of God's warning. His anger turned to murder. This does not sound like someone who knew and loved God as his loving Father, and from that relationship, wanted to please Him. Rather, it sounds like someone who was doing something *dutifully in order to receive affirmation* – with a religious spirit, if you like.

When God then questions Cain about Abel's disappearance, instead of falling on his face and admitting his guilt and asking for God's forgiveness for what he had done, (consider King David's response when the prophet Nathan called out his murderous sin), or even trying to explain what happened, he brushes it off with contempt.

> *"Then the Lord said to Cain, "Where is Abel your brother?" He said, "I do not know; am I my brother's keeper?"* - **Genesis 4:9-10 ESV**

Clearly, he was not in step with God. There was no acknowledging God as supreme - the one who is above all. Surely, he would have known even from Adam's accounts that God knew everything! To brush off God's question so contemptibly, indicates his heart was more for himself than for God, whereas Abel's actions demonstrate complete trust and love. True love gives and wants to please. Self-love wants to receive and give as little as possible. Clearly then, Cain only offered the sacrifice as an appeasement, or at most, as a dutiful offering that was action *without* heart.

Was Cain's attitude then the disqualifying factor? Cain had a **form of worship** but no love or heart felt praise for God.

Daniel I. Block wrote:

> "*We think that it is the sacrifice that makes the person acceptable to God; but actually, it is the person that makes the sacrifice acceptable.*"

The Scriptures agree:

> "*For the Lord sees not as man sees: man looks on the outward appearance, but the Lord looks on the heart.*"
> **-1 Samuel 16:7b ESV**

The problem with Cain's offering was not the offering itself, but Cain's heart. He had an outward appearance of worship, but inside his heart was tainted. God just wanted Cain's heart, but instead He was given "straw" (or whatever the crop happened to be.)

Now Hebrews states that *by **faith** Abel offered to God a better sacrifice than Cain*, (Hebrews 11:4). We might then be tempted to think that this statement in Hebrews just negates all I've discussed thus far. How does faith even relate to the heart? It relates in every way!

As I discussed in chapter one, faith is not simply repeating, "*I believe, I believe, I believe!*" like a mantra. That is not faith at all, but purely an effort to convince oneself that God will grant us what we have requested. You can't simply "will" faith into being. Nor do we automatically have faith because we are now Christians.

Rather, faith is born from the knowledge of who God is. It comes out of our *relationship* with Him. We don't just know about Him; we know Him. We know He is trustworthy. We know He is true to His promises and cares for our spiritual wellbeing. He cares for His sons and daughters. He will not abandon them nor leave them to struggle or suffer alone. We know this because we daily walk with Him. We have experienced His goodness and love towards us. It is a true "epignosis" – the Greek word meaning real and full intimate knowledge of God, and the word Paul uses in Philippians:

> "*And this I pray, that your love may abound still more and more in real knowledge and all discernment*" – **Philippians 1:9 - NASB**

We have faith because we know Him. It is a complete and real knowledge based not only on the Word of God but developed through our relationship, Holy Spirit revelations, and experience with Him. It is the difference between reading a book about someone, and knowing that someone on a personal and even "intimate" level. (In this case *spiritual* intimacy or closeness.)

Heart and faith *are* linked closely together, and therefore, Abel's faith had everything to do with his state of heart.

In John's first letter we read,

> "*We should not be like Cain, who was of the evil one and murdered his brother. And why did he murder him? Because his own deeds were evil and his brother's righteous.*" - **1 John 3:12 ESV**

Does this disagree with the verse in Hebrews we have mentioned previously? No! Let's compare the two.

> "*By* ***faith*** *Abel offered to God a more acceptable sacrifice than Cain, through which he* ***was commended as righteous****, God commending him by accepting his gifts. And through his faith, though he died, he still speaks.*" - **Hebrews 11:4 ESV**

The Hebrews explanation is that Abel was commended as righteous, because of his faith, and therefore his gifts were acceptable. In contrast, the state of Cain's heart and consequential lack of faith, earned him the title of the "*evil one*" according to John.

To sum up: It was Abel's *faith* that made his offering acceptable rather than his brother's. However, Abel faith was obviously *based upon* the revelation of who God really was, a heart knowledge gained through his *relationship* with Him. That is, because he knew and loved God, he gave ex travagantly. His faith action response to his love and trust in God, was to give his first lamb (and more besides because love gives), which also proved he trusted God would care for him even though his flock was now incomplete and the number of reproducing animals for the following year would be diminished. His heart had responded lovingly and with faith in God as his provider. Conversely, Cain's attitude was selfish and self-entitled, which indicates His love relationship with God was either shallow or non-existent.

This then made his sacrifice dutiful not from his heart, and thus, was unacceptable and even described as evil.

God wants us to delight in Him. He doesn't want lips service or mere works.

> "*These people draw near with their mouths and honour Me with their lips, but have removed their hearts far from Me.*" – **Isaiah 29:13 NKJV**

When we delight in Him, despite the darkness and turmoil surrounding us, it demonstrates our love and true faith in Him, and our worship becomes a sweet-smelling aroma to God.

He loves the smell of faith, especially the kind that delights in Him. In fact, Jesus commended people for their faith (the Centurion who asked for healing for his servant, the Syrophoenician woman whose daughter was possessed, the woman with the issue of blood, the leper left the others and returned to thank Jesus, and others). It showed Him that they truly understood who He was and that He had absolute power and authority to fulfil our every need. When we worship, we also tell God how great and able He is. In a sense it is a declaration of faith. He is God above all and He is able to do even the impossible!

Worship manifests the kind of faith that relaxes back in Jesus' arms and knows that the lover of our soul cares so much for us that He has the situation firmly in His hands and under His control.

.

Chapter 6

Guard Your Heart

~~~~~~~~~~~~~~~

Since love is a key to faith, it follows that if we want to maintain a lifestyle of faith, we must ensure that our hearts are not tainted by worldliness, (what goes in, is what comes out), and that we live holy and obedient lives to God.

Proverbs 4:23 makes it clear that to guard one's heart is vitally important. Let's also look at a few translations so that you can have a broader view of just what this text is saying.

> "*Above all else, **guard your heart**, for everything you do flows from it.*" – **NIV**

Other translations are as follows:

> "***Keep your heart** with all vigilance, for from it flow the springs of life.*" - **ESV**

> "***Guard your heart** above all else, for it determines the course of your life.*" - **NLT**

> "*Carefully **guard your thoughts** because they are the source of true life.*" - **CEV**

Or "The Passion Translation" puts' it this way:

> "*So above all, **guard the affections of your heart**, for they affect all that you are. Pay attention to the welfare of **your innermost being**, for from there flows the wellspring of life.*" - **TPT**

Dr Brian Simmons, the translator for the Passion Trans-
~~~~~~~~~~~~~~~

lation, adds this footnote:

> *"Although most translations "the issues of life," the Hebrew word, "**yasa**", is actually "seasons," especially springtime. Out of your heart flow the seasons of life. It is our hearts, not our ages or circumstances, that shape the seasons of our lives. If our hearts are tender to God, we can live in perpetual springtime."*

What does the Bible mean by our "heart"? Again, according to Dr Brian Simmons, the translator for the Passion Translation,

> "*The Hebrew word, "levav", is the most common word for "heart." It includes **our thoughts, our wills, our discernment, and our affections.***"

In fact, if you type in the word "Heart" into any online Bible, it will become quickly obvious that this is so – i.e. that the heart is the seat of our thoughts, will/motivation, and our emotions.

Here are just a few well-known verses which illustrate the various functions of the heart:

> "*Anxiety in the heart of man causes depression, but a good word makes it glad.*" – **Proverbs 12:25 NKJV**

> "*Before destruction the heart of a man is haughty, and before honour is humility*" – **Proverbs 18:12 NKJV**

> "*Delight yourself in the Lord and He shall give you the desires of your heart.*" - **Psalm 37:4 NKJV**

> "*But Mary kept all these things and pondered them in her heart.*" - **Luke 2:19 NKJV**

"Both the inward thought and the heart of man are deep." - **Psalm 64:6 NKJV**

"A merry heart does good, like medicine, but a broken spirit dries the bones." –**Proverbs 17:22 NKJV**

"A man's heart plans his way, but the LORD directs his steps." – **Proverbs 16:19 NKJV**

"Hope deferred makes the heart sick, but when the desire comes, it is a tree of life." – **Proverbs 13:12 NKJV**

"Eye has not seen, nor ear heard, nor have entered into the heart of man, the things which God has prepared for those who love Him." – **1 Corinthians 2:9 NKJV**

"So let each one give as he purposes in his heart, not grudgingly or of necessity; for God loves a cheerful giver." – **2 Corinthians 9:7 NKJV**

"The heart of the righteous studies how to answer, but the mouth of the wicked pours forth evil." – **Proverbs 15:28 NKJV**

"Wisdom rests in the heart of him who has understanding, but what is in the heart of fools is made known." – **Proverbs 14:33 NKJV**

Jesus, also spoke concerning the heart of man. It is the place where treasures are stored (Matthew 12:35; Luke 6:45),

"But those things which proceed out of the mouth ***come from the heart****, and they defile a man. For* ***out of the heart*** *proceed evil thoughts, murders, adulteries, fornications, thefts, false witness, blasphemies."* - **Matthew 15:18-19 NKJV**

That is: "things" that we have stored in our hearts are our attitudes and beliefs, and these motivate us to speak and act. Naturally, anything that motivates us, is critical to the way we live our lives.

Further, the state of our heart is the ultimate description of who we truly are,

> "*As in water face reflects face, so a man's heart reveals the man.*" - **Proverbs 27 19 NJKV**

> "*For as he thinks in his heart, so is he.*" - **Proverbs 23:7 NKJV**

We are expected to look more and more like Jesus throughout our lives. God is love. Since it is no longer I who live but Christ who lives in me, I should be looking more and more like "love". Does the state of our heart reflect this?

God expects us to:

> "*.... love the Lord your God with* ***all your heart*** *and with all your soul and with all your mind and with all your strength.*" - **Mark 12:30 ESV (See also Matt 22:37 & Luke 10:27**)

If God is not seated on the very throne in our hearts, in prior place, if we are number one in our lives, or if we have a creed rather than a relationship, we will fail to trust Him in times of crisis. We will endure for a time but ultimately give up because our faith rests in other things. Our hearts will fail because we choose to believe the circumstances, and the lies the enemy often envelopes around those events. We may hold on to His promises for a time, but eventually will succumb to disappointments and doubts. For this reason, guarding our heart is of utmost importance

- especially in times of trials! It is central to our faith and therefore, to endurance!

A guarded heart, is steadfast in the storms of life, because we know and therefore, have trust in the One whom we love. Nevertheless, if we do fail to hold on to faith - being beaten down by afflictions, or fail to love, or are so wounded we've shut our hearts down - the good news is that God is in the "heart restoration" business! Yes, we have a responsibility to guard our hearts diligently - to not let anything unGodly take root there, but when we are facing trials and our hearts are wounded, or fail from lack of strength, it is God who brings healing.

> "*Whom have I in heaven but You? And there is none upon earth that I desire besides You. My flesh and my heart fail; But God is the strength of my heart and my portion forever.*" - **Psalm 73:25-26 NKJV**

In fact, this is THE lesson that God wants us to learn: That in every situation we can trust Him with all we are because His love for us is enormous, true and unconquerable. When we eventually grasp the reality of this lesson, our hearts will be totally steadfast. Then when trials come:

> "*He will not be afraid of evil tidings; **His heart is steadfast, trusting in the LORD. His heart is established;** He will not be afraid*" - **Psalm 112:7-8 NKJV**

In conclusion to this discussion, guarding our hearts is not merely a matter of thinking good thoughts, but guarding our emotions, and motivations as well. That is, we must watch with vigilance the gates of our mind, our will and our emotions to prevent unwanted guests taking up residence there.

The Mind Gate

As mentioned, because we become what we think about ourselves, (i.e. "***For as he thinks in his heart, so is he.***" - Proverbs 23:7 NKJV) what we choose to think is important to our hearts and indicative of what we will become. This is why Paul instructs the Philippians,

> "*Finally, brothers, whatever is true, whatever is honourable, whatever is just, whatever is pure, whatever is lovely, whatever is commendable, if there is any excellence, if there is anything worthy of praise, think about these things.*" - **Philippians 4:8 ESV**

And again,

> "*Do not be conformed to this world, but be transformed by the renewal of your mind, that by testing you may discern what is the will of God, what is good and acceptable and perfect.*" - **Romans 12:2 ESV**

> "*Set your mind on things above, not on things on the earth.*" - **Colossians 3:2 NKJV**

What we read, hear, view, and then spend time thinking about, has the capacity to either shape us to look more like Jesus, ("And we all, who with unveiled faces contemplate the Lord's glory, are being transformed into his image with ever-increasing glory, which comes from the Lord, who is the Spirit." - 2 Corinthians 3:18 NIV - The word "contemplate" has the note: or "reflect" upon), or will conform us to the image of the world. Psalms reminds us,

> "*How can a young man keep his way pure? By guarding it according to your word. With my whole heart I seek you; let me not wander from your commandments! I*

have stored up your word in my heart, that I might not sin against you." - **Psalm 119:9-11 ESV**

Obviously, it is the Father's desire for us to be transformed to look like Jesus, not to look like the world. He is the Author and Finisher of our faith. He has not only saved us from eternal punishment, made us righteous through the blood of Jesus, given us a new life and a new identity through Him, and given us everything we need for life and Godliness (2 Peter 1:3), but He now shapes our character to look like Jesus, ready for eternity. In this endeavour, we have the choice and privilege to work alongside and partner with Him. Part of that work will include what we choose to put into our hearts and minds, and whom we choose to believe. We can transform our minds by filling them with what God says about us, and His instructions on how we should live - mostly by the Word of God - but also by meditating on good things as Paul describes, and the good examples of Godliness we witness in others.

If what we are feeding our heart does not fall into the description that Paul gives to the Philippians (above), I dare say, the things that flow out of our hearts will be rather tainted and more worldly than they should. Moreover, in times of crisis and trials, we will be more inclined to believe worldly opinions (which the devil often shapes to his own purposes) than God's.

Even though we may think we are very diligent with what we feed our minds, there are still times that the enemy will whisper thoughts into your minds - thoughts disguised as our own reckoning but designed especially to hit nerves and cause you to react. (A very low, dirty trick indeed.)

Remember that any hint of a lie mixed into the truth is still a lie, and any truthful fact that causes you to react negatively, is a seed for bad fruit to spring forth. Therefore, not all "truths" are good. This then calls for extra vigilance and discernment.

For example: Well before leaving Victoria, I had just visited a couple in the church in an effort to show Godly love and extend the hand of friendship to them. There was no other motive than that. However, this couple who were considered mature Christians, seemed very stand-offish, and non-reciprocating. Although I wondered about their cold reception, I was also contemplating how I might bridge the gap. Perhaps I could invite them to something other than simply dinner. Then as I was getting into the car to go after one such visit, I heard a voice say,

> *"They don't really like you!"*

Of course, I realised immediately that the thought had to have been from a demon, but I also realised that those words were true. (As I stated above, just because something is a true fact, doesn't automatically mean that it is good!) They didn't like me at all! Perhaps I was unintentionally offensive, talked too much, or just clashed with their personalities. Whatever the reason, I felt as if there was nothing that I could do to change the situation. They had made their feelings clear. It seemed so final! Needless to say, that that's about the time I stopped visiting and reaching out to them. As if bitten by the dog I was feeding, I decided it better to give no more, and not to try again. Instead of continuing to love, I closed my heart to them. Yes, it was totally the wrong choice!

My last example was not fuelled by fiery emotion as some thought darts, but it contained enough "truth" to for me to take notice, and my agreement with that "truth" gave it license to invade my thoughts and ultimately my heart as I began to feel a little wounded by the revelation. I failed to recognise the way the enemy was sneaking negativity into my heart.

So how can you tell the difference between a demon disguised as an angel of light and the voice of the Holy Spirit when the words that are spoken are actually facts or truths? My old pastor back in Ballarat use to tell us that when paper money was still in use, bank tellers were taught to find forgeries not by handling or examining the fake notes, but by handling the real notes, day in and day out. Then when the fake note came into the bank, they would easily recognise it - the feel of it, the weight of it, the smell of it, and even the look of it. It's the same with the thoughts that come into your mind. If you spend time in the word of God, in prayer and in His presence, the voice of the enemy is very easily distinguishable.

> *"But he who enters by the door is the shepherd of the sheep. To him the doorkeeper opens, and the sheep hear his voice; and he calls his own sheep by name and leads them out. And when he brings out his own sheep, he goes before them; and the sheep follow him, for they know his voice. Yet they will by no means follow a stranger, but will flee from him, for they do not know the voice of strangers." and "My sheep hear My voice, and I know them, and they follow Me."* - **John 10:2-5; 10:27 NKJV**

Knowing His voice will help you know the voices that are not God's quickly. I knew it had to be a demon. The problem was I **agreed** with what was said. Even if the revelation seems true, if it's from hell, we cannot afford to even contemplate it for a moment, let alone agree with it. Of course, 90% of what the enemy says will be exposed when held in the light of the Word of God, but if it does ring of truth, the potential fruit should be the final give away. What will the end result be if you acted this "truth"? It is important, therefore, that we do not agree with any thought other than God's. Better to brush it off instantly, than to give it access to your mind (thoughts) and ultimately your heart! As the saying goes, "*The birds may circle and try to land on your head, but you don't have to let then nest there.*"

Let's face it; you were designed to have Godly thoughts. 1 Corinthians 2:16 says that *we now have the mind of Christ*, and well able to hear and understand what the Holy Spirit teaches. We were created for this. Jesus said that another voice we will not follow (John 10:5 above). Why? Because we know the Master's voice and easily recognise other voices as not His.

This means that not only in everyday life but also in those times of crisis, the Holy Spirit can and does, bring to mind those Scriptures and testimonies we have meditated upon, both to encourage and to thwart the lies of the enemy. Because we have built up our faith - our trust and assurance in God - (Jude 1:20), we can endure any crisis and even praise God in the midst of the fire. We have armour coated our minds and hearts in the love and knowledge of who our God is and who we are in His sight.

The Emotional Gate

Thus far, I have discussed the mind and how important it is to think God's thoughts and not focus on what the enemy is doing. However, because the heart can be impacted and effected greatly by our thoughts, the things that motivate us, and emotions, it is equally important that we guard our emotions and our motivations as well.

Emotional Brusing & Hurts, & Unforgiveness

For example: when we are injured emotionally, we may have a tendency to want to get even, or at least to strike back. Following through with these negative emotions and subsequent thoughts and inclinations, only take us down the road of unforgiveness, bitterness and even to hate. These things ensnare our hearts because they are not of God but from hell itself! However, Jesus gives us the remedy:

> *"But I say to you, **love** your enemies, **bless** those who curse you, **do good** to those who hate you, and **pray** for those who spitefully use you and persecute you."* - **Matthew 5:44 NKJV**

> *"But I say to you who hear: **Love** your enemies, **do good** to those who hate you, **bless** those who curse you, and **pray** for those who spitefully use you."* - **Luke 6:27-28 NKJV**

That is: **love, bless, do good, and pray** for those who wrong us. These four essential ingredients create a shield for your heart when you are feeling hurt and unjustly wronged. Allowing negative emotions to fester, is a trap that only brings death. "Getting even" or silently despising another because of what they have done to us, will hurt us far more than the original infraction could ever do, because it not only corrupts our spirit, but can also cause bodily deterioration and medical conditions. See the previous chapter under the "Forgiveness" heading.)

While it's true that emotional wounding can really hurt us deeply and its effects can last for long periods of time, emotions can be healed and changed, using both psychological techniques, and more importantly, by the Holy

Spirit and through prayer. Handing over our hurts and brokenness to God brings wholeness and peace. After all, Jesus came to heal the broken hearted!

> "*The Spirit of the LORD is upon Me, Because He has anointed Me To preach the gospel to the poor; He has sent Me to* ***heal the broken hearted****, to proclaim liberty to the captives and recovery of sight to the blind, to set at liberty those who are oppressed; To proclaim the acceptable year of the LORD.*" - **Luke 4:18-19 NKJV**

He wants us to be totally pure of heart (mind, will & emotions), - to not harbour anything but love towards God and our fellow man.

> "*Blessed are the pure in heart, for they shall see God.*" - **Matthew 5:8 NKJV**

What's more, He will help us when this task seems almost impossible. He can take us to revisit those hurts and He can remove the pain from those memories, so that we can both heal and love unconditionally in return. What's more, there is a special grace available to us to both forgive and love unconditionally when we are emotionally wounded. All we have to do is give God the circumstances and the hurts and ask for His help - this grace. As we lean into Him in this way, He helps us through the pain to live as Jesus lived.

In my own case, after someone dear to me, deeply and utterly hurt me to the core (so much so that I thought if I went to bed that night, I wouldn't wake up the next day because it was so excruciatingly painful), I could have, in my humanness, turned on them in response. However, retribution is not God's way for His children, (God clearly states, "*Vengeance is Mine*" – Deuteronomy 32:35 and Romans 12:17-19) and instead, as I lifted the hurt to Him, God gave me the grace to embrace unconditional forgiveness, and also grace to love unconditionally, despite the constant and persistent pain I had to endure daily for about 5 years.

Why does God stipulate that vengeance is His and not ours? Afterall, those hurts and wrongs happened to us. It is because when we seek vengeance, not only are we not forgiving the other person in love, but it also hardens our hearts. Our mandate is to love above all. Okay, so that person may never change, but that's not our problem. We still need to love them in the same manner that God loved us, even while we were still sinners.

> "*But God demonstrates His own love toward us, in that while we were still sinners, Christ died for us.*" – **Romans 5:8 NKJV**

In another example, (and to be honest I can't remember the particulars of the incident as I dealt with the issue promptly and forgot them), someone from church wronged me in some way. Although I repeated often, "*I forgive them!*" negative thoughts kept plaguing me like a bunch of house flies that are determined to get into your eyes, nose and mouth. I'd forgive the person and lift the hurt to the Lord, only to have negative thoughts resurface again later, no matter how I tried to put them out of my mind. (To put this into perspective, this was not some deep seeded emotional hurt from my childhood that needed counselling, but a minor infraction on the part of another, that normally would not have been an issue apart from the interference from the enemy.) Subsequently, I was determined not to let these thoughts win, and continued to say, "*I forgive that person. It's over and done with, and now lies at the foot of the cross.*"

Then the following day before the church service began, I

was sitting quietly before the Lord trying to once again rid my mind of these negative thoughts, when I literally heard a voice scream into my ear, "*Harden your heart!*" Besides the fact that I just about jumped through the roof upon hearing it, I knew straight away that that voice was the voice of a demon. Because the enemy had inadvertently shown his hand, I was able to tell the demon to go, and there was peace! The voice completely stopped!

That wasn't quite the end of the matter though. Later in the service, the guest speaker prophesied over me, and his words began, "*Because you have not hardened your heart...*" God had turned an otherwise dangerous situation into a rewarding one. Choosing to forgive no matter what, guards your heart. Conversely, allowing our actions to be dictated to by the negative emotions does not just hurt another person and damage our relationship with them, but can be following the dictates of a demon rather than God. To whom do we belong? Our Father, King and Master is God, not the devil. We must be careful not to fall into the evil trap and do the devil's dirty work for him.

Strange Unexpected Emotions

Unfortunately, emotional wounding and unforgiveness are not the only emotions that the enemy uses to sneak passed our defences undetected, and these stealth emotions can equally poison our hearts. (For example, the feeling of entitlement when things don't turn out in our favour, or feeling we have been unjustly wronged, or think that people don't like us, or think that people are acting negatively towards us, just to name a few.) The enemy often employs emotionally loaded fiery darts that can set you ablaze if you do not quench them quickly. These new emotions have the potential to ruin relationships, and to cause great rifts with a lifetime of pain and regret. The trick is to recognise them in an instant so that you can extinguish them. That sounds great but how do you do that in practice?

Paul tells us that we can quench the fiery darts with the shield of faith.

> "*Above all, taking the shield of* ***faith*** *with which you will be able to quench all the fiery darts of the wicked one.*"
> **- Ephesians 6:16 NKJV**

There are many interpretations concerning the Christian armour as described by Paul. However, I tend to agree with those that interpret the armour to be a person's attitudes and standing in Christ. That is, we use the shield of *faith* by realising it is no longer I who lives but Christ who lives in me. That means I now have the mind of Christ, and all His thoughts are in agreement with His Word! I have the desires of Christ in my heart. Jesus doesn't ever have negative or wrongly placed emotions about anyone, for God is love and He is also just.

Therefore, I don't have to accept those emotions, especially if the fruit from them will be bad. I can know for sure that those thoughts and emotions are not mine but are from hell, and as such refuse to allow them our attention. This may mean we tell them aloud to take a hike, or quote Scriptures that refute them, or by declaring love and forgiveness or even blessing over someone who hurt us, or by worshipping God, or simply by just praying in tongues.

(The following example is an exert from my first book, "*Save Your Marriage*")

The manager of the business where I was working had just resigned, and the new guy had arrived to replace him. When I was first introduced, the thought popped into my head: "*He's a cutie!*" Now before I go further in this tale, please be aware that I don't weigh up the opposite sex in terms of cuteness. It's not my "thing" at all! Secondly, it was like someone had whispered in my ear and I was actually startled by the thought. It was obviously not my thought. At the time, I considered that that event was a very strange occurrence, but easily dismissing it, I went back to what I was working on and didn't give the incident another thought.

A few days passed. I was in my office this time when suddenly a thought of the new manager popped into my head, accompanied by a strong emotion of infatuation. Again, this made no sense whatsoever! I barely even knew this guy! Not only that, but I was *very* happy in my marriage at that time. I wasn't looking for another relationship, nor did I even want one. I loved my husband *and* my God too much to even consider it, and besides, I simply wasn't interested in this guy. This also had to be from the enemy. Nevertheless, even though I was able to rationalise this, the feelings remained. In response to this, I started praying in tongues and giving glory to God out loud. (I had a private office so I wasn't bothering anyone else.) Well, you guessed it, those feelings and emotions evaporated immediately - they were not *mine* to begin with. Not only that, but now exposed as fraudulent, those feelings did not return.

Disappointments

I suppose the above example was a somewhat obvious deception, but disappointments can be far less obvious. Now I have already discussed how disappointments can drain a person's faith away, but not to the extent of how they can mess with our hearts.

As we all know, disappointments are simply part of life. We

will all experience disappointments to some degree. However, we have a choice to dwell on our disappointments and the negative emotions attached to them, or to focus our attention back onto God's goodness, preferring instead to trust and have faith in Him and not the circumstances.

As briefly mentioned earlier, disappointments occur when a person's hopes and expectations (and attached to expectation is a certain amount of emotion whether they are well founded or not) are not met. The Bible reminds us:

> "*Hope deferred makes the heart sick, but when the desire comes, it is a tree of life.*" - **Proverbs 13:12 NKJV**

Disappointment is not a positive emotion. We can generally deal with the odd disappointment and move on, but when a person is constantly disappointed, the enemy can use those disappointments to covertly sneak into our heart unseen. Hidden under the feelings of disappointment can lie insidious temptations to doubt God, doubt His goodness and love, and can eventually lead to a complete loss of faith (as mentioned). Many that have walked that path, now believe that Christianity is merely some make-believe creed, that there is no God, and unfortunately, some of those people were even in ministry.

How did a string of disappointments become so powerful? They first captured the person's attention and then agreement, thereby empowering them. They entered the heart first through the emotions, which triggered other negative thoughts and emotions that justified them further. Because there was agreement, the enemy's lies were able to take root unhindered, and eventually the heart was poisoned. Finally, if there is sufficient wounding, an opportunistic spirit of grief can continue to do even more damage to the heart.

We may all experience, or at least be faced with, strong negative emotions biting at our hearts from time to time, but the important thing is to recognise that any negative emotion or inclination that is not rooted in love, is from hell. If we do not deal with these emotions immediately, they have the opportunity to mess with our thoughts while we try to make sense with them or try to justify them, thereby causing great damage to our hearts - especially if over time we unwittingly water those seeds via continued negative thoughts and actions that eventually produce an unGodly harvest!

The Motivational Gate

The final gate that requires our protection is our motivation or will. What are the things that really motivate us? What makes us get out of bed in the morning and behave the way we do? Are there beliefs about ourselves or the world, that cause us to seek after a certain path, goal or aspiration, and subsequently to behave a certain way? Motivation can often be insidious and sometimes the truth will lay buried beneath layers of habitualised behaviours and self-justifications. For example: If we do not really yet know the love of the Father, we may be fixated on making ourselves feel good about ourselves - a kind of self-medication with very nasty side effects. This will be the motivation behind whatever we do, whether it looks to the world to be altruistic or not.

If we view wealth and/or status as a way to feel good about ourselves, then it will colour all we do. If we believe that what people think about us is important to our happiness, then we will constantly be trying to make ourselves big in other people's eyes. If helping others makes us feel good about ourselves, then that will be our motivation to act kindly towards others, not their needs or love for them. Even in the church, if we are only doing to be seen, or doing because it makes us feel like good Christians, we are still motivated by the possibility of a "feel good about ourselves" outcome.

Most of us won't even stop to think why we do what we do. Our behaviour and reactions can be completely subconscious. For example: I love clothes and girly things and have had a very large wardrobe ever since I was able to buy my own things. On seeing it for the first time, a non-Christian friend once made the remark,

"*You're obviously making up for something!*"

Perhaps not the sweetest words ever spoken but they did hold an air of truth. I can't say I'd ever thought about it that way, but never ever having had the affirmation of my earthly father, I was unconsciously trying to make myself feel okay about myself. If I could at least look good, I would feel there was something likeable about me. I hadn't even thought about it before, but that motivation was not Godly and yet had lain hidden in my heart for years. Thankfully, now I know I am totally loved by God and although I still like to look my best, do not need this in order to feel worthy or okay as a human being.

Some deep-seated motivations can originate from childhood trauma, and may require Christian counselling where the loving hand of the Father can heal and change, but then there are those that merely colour our decisions every day. If we were to stop and ask why, those motivations would be very apparent. Why do we put our hands up for ministry? Is it because we love the church and people and wish to serve, or because we are hoping to be noticed and promoted, or perhaps even to convince ourselves that we are good Christians? Why do we run to see the next greatest prophetic speaker to visit town? Is it because of our love for the presence of God and to hear Him speak, or are we hoping to receive another prophetic word to make ourselves feel good about ourselves?

Remember Corinthians 13:1-3, that without love as our motivation we are nothing and what we do amounts to nothing.

> "*Though I speak with the tongues of men and of angels, but have not love, I have become sounding brass or a clanging cymbal. And though I have the gift of prophecy, and understand all mysteries and all knowledge, and though I have all faith, so that I could remove mountains, but have not love, I am nothing. And though I bestow all my goods to feed the poor, and though I give my body to be burned, but have not love, it profits me nothing.*" - **1 Corinthians 13:1-3 NKJV**

Wow! That means that knowing our motivation is not just important but *imperative*! If we are not **motivated by our love for God first and foremost** and as a result, love for others, **not only will the works we do be counted as nothing, but we will also be unrecognisable as belonging to Him**. Are not Jesus's disciples recognised by their love?

This motivation gate, is much harder to guard, and if we are not vigilant, can allow the enemy to subversively taint our heart. Paul tells the Corinthians to examine themselves.

> "*Examine yourselves, to see whether you are in the faith. Test yourselves. Or do you not realize this about yourselves, that Jesus Christ is in you? - unless indeed you fail to meet the test!*" - **2 Corinthians 13:5 ESV**

Paul was talking about doing what was right before God (vs. 7) but if our motivation is not love, what we've done is not a matter of right or wrong but it is absolutely of no value at all (1 Cor 13)! Further, if God has not sanctioned our actions, they are worthless before God and could even be detrimental long term. In fact, any works we lay on the foundation of our salvation that are not ordained by God, will be burned up as stubble.

> "*According to the grace of God which was given to me, as a wise master builder I have laid the foundation, and another builds on it. But let each one take heed how he builds on it. For no other foundation can anyone lay than that which is laid, which is Jesus Christ. Now if anyone builds on this foundation with gold, silver, precious stones, wood, hay, straw, each one's work will become clear; for the Day will declare it, because it will be revealed by fire; and the fire will test each one's work, of what sort it is. If anyone's work which he has built on it endures, he will receive a reward. If anyone's work is burned, he will suffer loss; but he himself will be saved, yet so as through fire.*" - **1 Corinthians 3:10-15 - NKJV**

If you find it hard to ask yourself the "*What is motivating me to want to do that?*" question, having someone you trust ask the question (e.g. Christian mentor or close Christian friend), can also shine a light on your heart. Ultimately though, your relationship with God, coupled with a daily examination while you sit quietly before Him, is the best place to find the reality of your heart. The Holy Spirit knows all and will thankfully not allow us to "get away with" anything. He is the author and finisher of our faith, and knows exactly how to teach us the way that best suits us!

My old pastor from Ballarat use to say that when we are

first saved, we are clean, feeling loved and happy, but although we've been washed in the blood, our character (which is seated in our heart) still needs a great deal of work. We may not even realise it. It's almost as if God has His hand over it, in case we'd be overwhelmed with all the traits and flaws that need adjusting or eradicating. However, at the right time He moves His hand just a little and points to an issue with our character. Unlike the enemy who whispers thoughts enflamed with emotion, when the Holy Spirit reveals to us character flaws embedded in our heart (something which taints our motivations), there is no strong emotion or judgement or condemnation attached. We simply see this revelation for what it is and can answer calmly, "*Oh yeah! I am like that, aren't I?*" or "*Yes, that really was my motivation. I see that now!*" Thus, the process of change can begin.

Interconnection: Mind, Will & Emotions, & Their Fruit

These three areas that affect our heart often without us realising it, will ultimately give birth to actions.

Negative thoughts can stir up negative emotions, which can affect what we believe and motivate us to behave negatively and in a very unGodly fashion.

Negative emotions that occurred because of some incident, or even tragedy, can cause us to agree with them and then in turn to *think negatively* (about others, or even negate *beliefs* about ourselves which were true). These new negative beliefs in turn will affect or motivate how we *respond/act*.

Negative *beliefs* and motivations can produce actions that conjure false emotions. That is, we may feel better about ourselves afterwards, but this is only short lived, and in the end will cause us to repeat the cycle, never ever finding true satisfaction. (Example: Addictions and impulsive behaviours that produce some momentary satisfaction but produce a long-term negative result.)

As we've already discussed, if our actions are not birthed in love, they are nothing, and can even give us a false sense of security. If on the other hand, what we do is out of the overflow of our love for God, (and that includes a loving response of obedience to what He might ask us to do), life will issue forth. From loving obedience, salvations and the miraculous may flow, and ultimately, at the end of the age, the God who knows us and who sees all, will reward our loving service.

Temptations

I have briefly given you an overview of the gates to the heart, but the enemy of our souls can sneak through those gates via temptations, and they can be so disguised that we don't realise what we allow to pass. A bit like a robber hiding under a blanket as the cart is wheeled through the gate to the city.

For example: God or one of His prophets may give the message that God is about to move us into a new ministry, or season, or location, or even that He is about to bless us enormously. This thought is very appealing - even exciting! Wow! That's great! We feel good about it! It has peeked our emotions. How will this happen? We might begin to plan and spend hours thinking about the details, and searching for the right books, tools, house/location or whatever. We may imagine what the blessing is like or if financial, how we would spend it. After all, we just want to be prepared, right? However, we can be tempted to give that new thing too much attention, thus, making it an idol which consumes our thoughts and the desires of our heart. Even our prayers can be distracted by this, or centred around this rather than asking the Holy Spirit how to pray.

This temptation entered through the emotion gate and we didn't see it. It then began manipulating our thoughts and motivations. Anything that takes our eyes off God has the potential to poison our heart against Him. You could call this temptation "*the lust of our eyes*"!

Another example: Being physically exhausted, and too tired to do much else, or even being ill and unable to do much at all, we may be tempted to simply put our feet up and watch our favourite show. Now the show may be very wholesome and even Christian - and there are now plenty of good Christian TV series and movies available - but is this beneficial? How is it affecting our thought processes? Is this a positive thing? Is God happy for us to use our time in this manner or are there more pressing things He has for us to do (perhaps calling, encouraging or even witnessing to someone), even if those things are simply to sit with Him in prayer or worship, or study the Word? In truth, we still belong to Him, no matter how we feel. (i.e. Although He cares about our wellbeing - even our tiredness, being tired is not a "do-whatever-you-feel-like-doing" free pass! He may just be saying to put on some worship music and rest in Him!) Jesus was physically hungry at the end of His 40-day fast in the desert, but He chose not to change the stones into bread when tempted. He did not give into the flesh at all! This temptation to indulge the flesh instead of asking God what He wants us to do, even if we are tired out, can be considered "*the lust of our flesh*". (I'm sure you can think of far worse examples in this category.)

Yet another example: If we receive a major blessing or opportunity, and are not guarding our hearts, we may be tempted to believe we deserved this because we are more holy, more giving or just better than others. Such a seemingly positive event can have very negative consequences for our hearts!

A variation on this theme is in making a choice for something "life-changing" (be it a job, ministry, business deal or whatever that we think may be "the one chance in a lifetime" that we feel will benefit us), when in actual fact, God is trying to steer us away from this because it will not ultimately be beneficial to us. We can even justify our choice by calling it God's blessing. After all, He is good to His children, right? However, to state the obvious, God's idea of what is good for us can differ greatly to our own. Nevertheless, our desires can over-ride His warnings when we keep focussed on satisfying them, instead of focussed on God.

These kinds of temptations are known as "*the pride of life*". We might be inclined to tell ourselves that pride is easily avoidable, and hey, we've gotten that beat. We don't walk around puffed up or talk about ourselves and how wonderful we are, but no, pride can sometimes be subtle and come disguised in any number of positive events, promotions, gifts and surprises.

Remember that Jesus was likewise tempted in the desert. Each temptation was a picture of the lust of the eyes, the lust of the flesh and the pride of life. In a similar manner, we too will be tempted in these areas. Do we know our Scriptures well enough to combat these temptations (when we recognise them) with a similar reply Jesus gave to the tempter, "*It is written....*"

Some temptations are obvious; others we may not recognise until the Holy Spirit stops us abruptly and points to the state of our heart. This is why vigilance is required, and why Paul suggests that we guard with all diligence!

Chapter 7:
Faith Builders

~~~~~~~~~~~~~~~

As we have discussed thus far, our faith is built upon our knowledge of Him through our relationship with Him. However, that's only part of the story. We can also know Him through His Word.

Knowing God's Word - Knowing God

It is amazing that so many Christians rely on their Sunday sermon to get their weekly dose of the word of God. I'd like to take a look at a very difficult passage of Scripture to illustrate the importance of knowing Jesus through His Word.

I want to discuss John 6. Jesus had just fed the five thousand, dismissed the crowd, sent His disciples away by boat while He went to the mountain to pray, and then later seeing them struggling against the wind and waves from five miles away (that must have been supernatural vision), came to them walking across the water. We all know the story.

The following day, the crowds returned hoping to get another free lunch, but when they couldn't find Jesus or His disciples, they went to Capernaum looking for Him. Because this is a long passage, I encourage you to read it for yourself, but I will list the main points for you. Let's start from verse 25.

When they discovered Jesus in Capernaum, they asked how He had travelled there, but Jesus calls out their motive straight away – they came looking for another free lunch.
~~~~~~~~~~~~~~~

After revealing this, Jesus instructed them to seek heavenly food that the Son of Man gives instead.

They basically then demanded He prove to them He was the Son of Man - do something miraculous. Jesus responds by saying that's not how it works, you have to believe on Him. Hearing this they then asked for a sign. Moses gave them manna to eat every day for 40 years! Could He top that?

Jesus corrected them. God gave the manna, not Moses. However, God also gives them the true bread from heaven, and that bread is the One whom the Father sent to them. Sounded great to them. They wanted *that* bread, but they failed to understand that bread was Jesus, and only He could feed them spiritually so that they could have eternal life through Him.

Then Jesus told them plainly that He was/is the bread of life. He who comes to Him will never be hungry and he who believes in Him will never thirst. However, He also explained that even though they had seen Him, (and had witnessed and experienced all those miraculous things He had done), they still did not believe, for they hadn't *really* seen Him. Their spiritual eyes were not opened. Note, that Jesus said in verse 40, "*that everyone who sees the Son and believes in Him may have everlasting life*" However, all they could see were the physical benefits they could gain if they hung around this man. They were merely "*hangers on*".

Jesus only did the will of the Father, and consequently, would receive only those that the Father had chosen (cf. John 6:37, 44, 65) for Him, and none of them would be cast out. He had come to do the Father God's will, which was to lose no one, but to raise them up on the last day. Thus, God has ordained that anyone who *sees* and believes in Jesus, may have everlasting life and be raised up on the last day.

Unfortunately, the religious complained about Jesus referring to Himself as the “bread from heaven”, and reminded Jesus that they knew Joseph and Mary, His parents, thus, He could hardly say He came from heaven!

Jesus doesn’t try to answer this, but continues to speak the truth that no one can come to Him unless the Father who sent Him, firstly draws Him.

They don’t know the Father, but He did, because He has seen Him face to face, and come from Him. Therefore, His testimony is far more reliable than their earthly observations. What Jesus was telling them was absolute truth! While it is true that their ancestors ate manna in the desert, they all died. However, the bread (i.e. Jesus), that came down from heaven, would produce in those who believed, everlasting life.

Jesus them tells them this spiritual truth: He is the Living Bread from heaven. Eat this bread and you’ll have everlasting life. What’s more, the “bread” He was referring to was His flesh which He would give for the life of the world. (Reference to the crucifixion).

The Jews totally missed the point Jesus was making. They thought He was telling them to literally eat His flesh and blood and complained about this. However, for those not hungry for God, the truth of this was obscured. It needed to be revealed by the Holy Spirit! Thus, those truly seeking after Him would understand. Subsequently, Jesus does not try to explain, but rather told them that if they do not eat His flesh and drink His blood, they would have no spiritual life in them. Those that do, would have eternal life and would be raised on the last day. What’s more, those people would abide in Him and He in them. It's not like the manna that the fathers ate and died. This is living bread from heaven, that gives everlasting life.

Upon hearing this, they were totally confused. They'd totally missed the spiritual truth hidden in these words. How could they possibly eat His flesh and drink His blood? Knowing who was complaining about this, Jesus asked if they were offended by this. Would it be any different then, if they were to see the most amazing miracles of heaven? Probably not, as their spiritual eyes were closed, and so were their hearts.

Then Jesus clarifies His whole argument, but by this stage, they had already turned completely away in their hearts.

> "*It is the **Spirit** who gives life; the flesh profits **nothing**. The **WORDS** that I speak to you are **spirit, and** they are **life**. But there are some of you who do not believe." For Jesus knew from the beginning who they were who did not believe, and who would betray Him.*"
> – **John 6:63,64 NKJV**

Note that it states that Jesus knew who the non-believing "hangers on" were, for no one can come to Jesus without the Father's say so. Therefore, those disciples left Jesus and walked with Him no more, and Jesus did not try to prevent them. Nevertheless, to those who stayed, (namely the twelve) He asked if they wanted to go too. The response was beautiful and showed that Peter understood even in part:

> "*But Simon Peter answered Him, 'Lord, to whom shall we go? You have the words of eternal life. Also, we have come to believe and know that You are the Christ, the Son of the living God.'*" – **John 6:69 NKJV**

The "bread" is the Words of Jesus, the Son of God.

OK. What does that have to do with faith? Those that know the word, know Jesus for He is the "Living Word". The Bible isn't just an inspired word. It is living and active, and sharper than any two-edged sword.

> *"For the word of God is living and powerful, and sharper than any two-edged sword, piercing even to the division of soul and spirit, and of joints and marrow, and is a discerner of the thoughts and intents of the heart."* – **Hebrews 4:12 NKJV**

John (1 John 1:1) describes Jesus as the Word of Life, and that the word *was* God (John 1:1). Paul also instructs the Philippians to be blameless and hold fast to the Word of *life*, that they may rejoice in the day of Christ, (Philippians 2:16).

This Word, Jesus, the Son of God, now lives in you. As you study His word, there is an activation and spiritual response that brings revelation and spiritual growth and transformation, for as we behold Him, we are transformed into His image (2 Corinthians 3:18) from glory to glory. We begin to understand more about who God is and why He does what He does. We understand why it's important to follow Him and believe on Him, for He is always right, and His words have always proven to be absolute truth!

Without a relationship with God, it is possible to read the Bible and not see the truth it reveals, just as those that followed Jesus in the flesh heard His words and still failed to understand the spiritual truths they contained. Many non-Christians have read the Bible looking for something to prove their point. It's just like reading a book to them. However, there are also some hungry hearts that may not be saved, that have been transformed by these words, because the Father has already chosen them. These Biblical words are impregnated with Holy Spirit revelation, which sinks deep onto their hearts and brings conviction and change.

As Christians, it's amazing just what happens when we actually deliberately make take time to study the word under the guidance of the Holy Spirit. Just an hour per day will change your Christian Walk. You'll begin to see things differently. Scripture verses will appear to jump off the page and hit your heart, other related Scripture verses will come to mind, not just at that time but at just the right time need them, and you will begin to understand. You'll also begin to hear with accuracy as the Holy Spirit speak s to you throughout the day, and you'll have the words you need to pray for others as He intercedes through you. It's like your spiritual ears suddenly improves like never before, and your spiritual eyesight begins to see things you never thought possible.

The word is therefore, integral to building up your faith. The Holy Spirit's revelation will open your eyes to the true character of God. He is good, generous and kind to His children and He is completely trust worthy. The more you see Him, the more faith you will have in Him.

Dying to Self & Separation unto Him

This is something the church does not talk about often. It can be a hard topic to broach as many don't like the thought of holiness, and berate pastors who try to teach this aspect of the Word of God. It is somewhat like children, who want to be fed the blessings and the feel-good moments without having to feed themselves and/or without helping/giving to others. This kind of "faith" is only as good as their feeling of well-being is high. As such, I have heard some horrendous stories about "believers" "exploring their faith" in sinful activities. We were saved unto righteousness, not so that we could continue in the same life style as we once did, but for His glory.

Whatever, your personal view on this matter, the Bible clearly states that we are to be Holy just as the Father is Holy.

> "*For I am the Lord who brought you up from the land of Egypt to be your God; thus,* ***you shall be holy, for I am holy.***" – **Leviticus 11:45 NKJV**

> "*Speak to all the congregation of the sons of Israel and say to them,* ***'You shall be holy, for I the Lord your God am holy.***" - **Leviticus 19:2 NKJV**

> "*As He who called you is holy, you also be holy in all your conduct, because it is written,* ***"Be holy, for I am holy.***" – **1Peter 1:15,16 NKJV**

> "*Therefore, having these promises, beloved, let us cleanse ourselves from all filthiness of the flesh and spirit,* ***perfecting holiness*** *in the fear of God.*" – **2Corinthians 7:1 NKJV**

> "*...just as He chose us in Him before the foundation of the world, that we* ***should be holy*** *and without blame before Him in love*" – **Ephesians 1:4 NKJV**

> "*...and that you put on the new man which was created according to God, in true righteousness and* ***holiness.***" – **Ephesians 4:24 NKJV**

> "*Finally, then, brethren, we urge and exhort in the Lord Jesus that you should abound more and more, just as you received from us how you ought to walk and to*

please God; for you know what commandments we gave you through the Lord Jesus. For this is the will of God, your sanctification: that you should abstain from sexual immorality; that each of you should know how to possess his own vessel in sanctification and honour, not in passion of lust, like the Gentiles who do not know God; that no one should take advantage of and defraud his brother in this matter, because the Lord is the avenger of all such, as we also forewarned you and testified. ***For God did not call us to uncleanness, but in holiness****. Therefore, he who rejects this does not reject man, but God, who has also given us His Holy Spirit.*" – **1Thessalonians 4:1-7 NKJV**

"*And everyone who has this hope in Him* ***purifies himself, just as He is pure.***" – **1 John 3:3 NKJV**

This is only a smattering of the Bible verses calling God's people to be holy (i.e. separated from the sinful activities of the world). There are many more! Pauls also warns the Galatians that those who deliberately sin will not see the kingdom of God, and then spells out exactly what he means by sin:

"*Now the works of the flesh are evident, which are: adultery, fornication, uncleanness, lewdness, idolatry, sorcery, hatred, contentions, jealousies, outbursts of wrath, selfish ambitions, dissensions, heresies, envy, murders, drunkenness, revelries, and the like; of which I tell you beforehand, just as I also told you in time past, that those who practice such things* ***will not inherit the kingdom of God.***" – **Galatians 5:19-21 NKJV**

The writer of Hebrews also warns that without holiness, no one will see God,

"*Pursue peace with all people, and* ***holiness, without which no one will see the Lord.***" – **Hebrews 12:14 NKJV**

Yes, we were made righteous by the blood of Jesus at salvation, but that on-going walk of salvation should reflect **His** righteousness, because as we look to Him, we are transformed more into His image (2Cor 3:18). Wilful sin mirrors the enemy, not Jesus, and indicates the kind of relationship we have with God, and thus, the true faith we actually have in Him.

Whatever way you want to look at it, as Christians, we cannot ignore the call to be holy. It is clearly spelt out in the word of God. We don't have the luxury of doing *some* of His commands and not the rest. We can't just take the benefits and ignore the responsibilities of obedience and holiness! If we do ignore holiness, aren't we just being hypocritical and a modern-day "hanger on" as well? If we truly love God above all else, we will want to please Him – bottom line.

How then, can we remain holy – a people set apart? How can we avoid being caught up in sin in such a sinful world? As mentioned previously, Paul also instructs us to walk in the Holy Spirit. The Holy Spirit is grieved by sin, but if we are willing to follow *His* lead, to make *the choice* to separate our hearts from worldly things and give our all to God, we will not satisfy the lusts of the flesh.

"*I say then: Walk in the Spirit, and you shall not fulfill the lust of the flesh.*" - **Galatians 5:16 NKJV**.

Obedience sometimes demands that we silence the flesh, even if it kicks and screams and insists that it doesn't want to do this. We may not want to pray, read our Bible, spend time in worship, or just spend time with God, but when we make a good habit of these things, we develop a greater hunger for them, and for that closeness with God.

Easier said than done when starting from a distant place in your heart! This is why God has made our salvation experience akin to falling in love. Many of us have experienced a kind of euphoria when we first meet Jesus at salvation. Loving God was wonderful. It was effortless to spend time with Him because we were so enraptured by Him. From that place we were called to deeper intimacy, and heart knowledge of Him. However, sometimes life gets in the way, and hearts become dry. It's then that choice to draw close to Him in love and be obedient, will demand that great sacrifices be made. That is, His will above mine no matter the cost. Jesus gave us this example in Gethsemane,

> "*Father, if it is Your will, take this cup away from Me; nevertheless, not My will, but Yours, be done*" – **Luke 22:42 NKJV**

> "*O My Father, if it is possible, let this cup pass from Me; nevertheless, not as I will, but as You will.*" – **Matthew 26:39 NKJV**

It is a sacrifice to choose Jesus and His will first. Jesus knows this – He already made the ultimate sacrifice for us! Therefore, Paul also tells us that this kind of sacrifice is reasonable for all Christians.

> "*Therefore, I urge you, brothers and sisters, by the mercies of God, to present your bodies [dedicating all of yourselves, set apart] as a living sacrifice, holy and well-pleasing to God, which is your rational (logical, intelligent) act of worship.*" – **Romans 12:1 AMP**

I have used the Amplified version here as it does a great job of bringing out the meaning in the translation. It is only logical, rational, and reasonable that any Christian puts God's will before their own. It's a sacrifice of our will and demands things that we may simply not want to do or give – things that cost physically, financially, mentally, and in time. (For example: going out of your way to visit someone you wouldn't associate with in the natural, to show God's love, possibly meet some physical needs they have, and share life with them.)

Again, how does this relate to faith? I spoke at length about disobedience in the "*Hinderances to Faith*" chapter, and described how disobedience shifts our focus off Jesus, and on to self. It quenches our ability to hear the Holy Spirit, and our ability to see the deep spiritual revelations and truths he is trying to give to us. We see God less and less as we sin, and as a result, our ability to have faith in Him also dwindles.

Conversely, as we separate ourselves from sin, dying to selfishness, and dedicating ourselves to follow Him in purity and holiness, all the other voices begin to fade. We hear Him above the noise of this world, and the word begins to take on a clarity we had never seen before. When this happens, we also see God with more clarity and thus, our faith in Him will also rise.

The Words of Testimony

> "*And they overcame him by the blood of the Lamb and by the word of their testimony, and they did not love their lives to the death.*" – **Revelation 12:11 NKJV**

Hearing testimonies, builds faith. If God can do it for others, He can do it for us too. This also helps to keep the enemies lies at bay. The enemy loves to whisper that God doesn't love us, won't answer our prayers, or that we are the dregs of Christendom. However, these are all lies. Hearing someone else who is in the same boat as you, tell how Jesus came through for them, instantly cuts through the lies and helps us realise we can have faith to see the same result. The enemy has been overcome by the words of testimony, and faith has been built up.

This is why pastors and preachers often tell stories and give testimonies of the marvellous things God has done – especially during healing and miracle services. They want you to take your eyes off the problem and see again how good God really is and how He wants to do the same for you.

Worship

I won't rehash what I have already stated in the "*Intimacy*" chapter, other than reminding you that drawing close to God in worship enables us to see Him as He is – His character, His great love for us, His reliability, His truthfulness and so on. On these things we can securely and confidently base our faith. It is in worship, as we fix our eyes on Him, that the worries of this world begin to take a shadowy second place, and we relax knowing He's bigger, and He's got this! It is a reminder that nothing is impossible for our God!! (Matthew 19:26; Mark 10:27; Luke 1:37)

Worship is for our benefit. We sing out loud His glorious attributes, all the things He's done for us, and all His promises that are awaiting us. These things are faith building and aligning. They put the facts straight in our minds, replacing lies with truths.

Worship loudly tells the enemy what the truth of the situation is, and that what he's been trying to feed us is mere deception. Any wonder he hates it. It undermines his work!

The Encouragement of Others

> "*He who says he is in the light, and hates his brother, is in darkness until now. He who loves his brother abides in the light, and there is no cause for stumbling in him. But he who hates his brother is in darkness and walks in darkness, and does not know where he is going, because the darkness has blinded his eyes.*" – **1John 2:9-11 NKJV**

Reaching spiritual maturity requires **mutual support and encouragement**. Being with others gives us new views and insights. It makes us understand faith better.

Celebrating each other's kingdom wins through the power of God, motivates us to keep going. This support boosts our growth and strengthens our community. It helps us reach the goals mentioned in Ephesians 4:13.

Paul also tells the Thessalonian church to encourage each other and build each other up. Build-up in what? Faith!

> "*Therefore encourage one another and build each other up, just as in fact you are doing.*" – **1 Thessalonians 5:11 NIV**

> "*And let us consider one another in order to stir up love and good works, not forsaking the assembling of ourselves together, as is the manner of some, but exhorting one another, and so much the more as you see the Day approaching.*" – **Hebrews 10:24-25 NKJV**

> "*Do not let any unwholesome talk come out of your*

mouths, but only what is helpful for building others up according to their needs, that it may benefit those who listen." – **Ephesians 4:29 ESV**

Paul even sent Timothy to build up the Thessalonian's faith, because he feared that without the correct encouragement and faith building, they may be deceived and tempted to lose faith.

"...and sent Timothy, our brother and minister of God, and our fellow labourer in the gospel of Christ, to establish you and encourage you concerning your faith" **– 1 Thessalonians 3:2 NKJV**

The encouragement of the brethren and sharing of sound doctrines, testimonies and revelations from God's word, helps us to recognise the deceptions and false teachings of the enemy.

"Without counsel, plans go awry, but in the multitude of counsellors they are established." – **Proverbs 15:22 NKJV**

"Where there is no counsel, the people fall; but in the multitude of counsellors there is safety." – **Proverbs 11:14 NKJV**

There is value in having many wise counsellors in Christ, and in sharing revelation. (However, this of course, requires discernment when choosing to whom you will listen. Suffice to say, your pastors and church leaders should be responsible in this matter.) Good counsel and encouragement, protects us, and boosts both our faith in God and what He can do. Encouraging one another helps us to stay true to what we believe and to stand firm in our faith in God.

Together we keep each other on the straight and narrow and dispel the lies the enemy whispers about ourselves and about God. It sheds light on the truth, and safeguards us against from losing faith.

Loving The Brethren

When we love our brethren, it is a testimony to, and of the kind of, faith we have in God. James says that if we truly have faith, we will have the works to prove it.

> "*But someone will say, "You have faith, and I have works." Show me your faith without your works, and I will show you my faith by my works.*" – **James 2:18 - NKJV**

Our acts of love towards our brethren prove our faith in God. It is out of the overflow of our love for God that works appear. We want to do those things He wants us to do, and to love those who are dear to Him. Therefore, works are a practical demonstration of our faith in God.

Further, our obedience to God is a demonstration that we love God. (I mentioned this already in a previous chapter.) There are other Scripture verses stating the same thing, especially the words of Jesus in John 14:15, but I think John also sums it up nicely when he wrote,

> "*But those who obey God's word truly show how completely they love Him. That is how we know we are living in Him.*" – **1 John 2:5 NKJV**

Jesus demonstrated His love when He went to the cross in complete obedience to the Father, not because He wanted to do so. In fact, He asked the Father if that cup of suffering could pass by. Nevertheless, He added, that He wanted to do the Father's will rather than His own. Why? Because He loved the Father and wanted the world to see what that looked like.

> "*I don't have much more time to talk to you, because the ruler of this world approaches. He has no power over me, but I will do what the Father requires of me, so that the world will know that I love the Father.*" – **John 14:30-31 NKJV**

This then, is the perfect example for us. Do we love our brethren enough to die in their place? Jesus commanded that we love one another as He loved,

> "*A new commandment I give to you, that you love one another; as I have loved you, that you also love one another. By this all will know that you are My disciples, if you have love for one another.*" – **John 13:34,35 NKJV**

When He said, "you are My disciples" (above), it indicated He was talking about His followers, or if you want that current for today, members of His church. Consider this, if a gunman walked into the church and threatened to kill every member of the congregation unless someone volunteered to die for the rest, would you be willing to raise your hand and volunteer? That's a sobering thought. Do I really love my brethren that much? Yet, Jesus died in our place. That's love!

If we love as He loved, we fulfil the law of love (i.e. to love one another as He loved us), and we demonstrate that we truly love God. Love is the foundation of our faith. Thus, loving the brethren is not only proof of our love for God, it is also fundamental to our faith!

Further, when we love the brethren, we will eventually see

the fruit of this love, as we encourage our brethren to go further and grow in God, and see His promises come to pass in their lives. This then, encourages us in our faith in God as well. It becomes a win-win situation.

Stirring up the Joy

Even the word "*delight*" in the verse from Psalm 37:4, suggests a we make a conscious effort to rejoice. The Psalmists and Old Testament prophets alike, often encouraged their readers to rejoice in God. Paul also instructs us to rejoice in Philippians (see Philippians 3:1, 4:4). Why? When we laugh, even in the face of adversity, it demonstrates a certain amount of assurance that the outcome will be positive despite the way things appear. Why? Because He's got this! We have faith in God that He will cause all things to turn for our good. Therefore, we can simply relax, lean back into His strong arms, and enjoy the ride.

> "*And we know that all things work together for good to those who love God, to those who are the called according to His purpose.*" – **Romans 8:28 NKJV**

God is pleased by this kind of demonstrable faith and trust in Him. It is character building for us.

> "*My brethren, count it all joy when you fall into various trials knowing that the testing of your* ***faith*** *produces patience.*" – **James 1:2,3 NKJV**

This kind of joy spills over into all that we do for Him as demonstrated by the Macedonian believers, who

> "*In a great trial of affliction, the abundance of their joy and their deep poverty abounded in the riches of their liberality.*" – **2 Corinthians 8:2 NKJV**

When we are joyful, we will also abound in hope:

> *"Now may the God of hope fill you with all joy and peace in believing, that you may abound in hope by the power of the Holy Spirit."* – **Romans 15:13 NKJV**

(Note: I have already discussed how hope and faith are interconnected in the previous chapters.) Further, joy is a manifestation of those who are children of His Kingdom.

> *"The kingdom of God is not eating and drinking, but righteousness and peace and joy in the Holy Spirit."* – **Romans 14:17 NKJV**

You might be thinking, that you can't just rejoice and that it depends on one's circumstance. However, that is not correct. If it is commanded in the Scriptures over and over, you obviously can. It simply demands and attitude shift and our focus to become totally fixed on Him, all He has done, and all He promised to do.

> *"But let all those rejoice who put their trust in You; Let them ever shout for joy, because You defend them; Let those also who love Your name Be joyful in You."* – **Psalm 5:11 NKJV**

It has been said that Smith Wigglesworth did a little happy dance in his private space each day, in order to stir himself up in the Lord and rejoice in Him, because this set His focus and trust where it needed to be – upon God alone. It is often a decision to be joyful, sometimes even sacrificial in that we may not feel like rejoicing.

> *"I will offer sacrifices of joy in His tabernacle; I will sing, yes, I will sing praises to the LORD."* – **Psalm 27:6b NKJV**

Nevertheless, God delights in us as we delight in Him. Moreover, as we choose to draw close, and demonstrate our love for Him though our joyful obedience, He often shares His joy with us. It's a supernatural joy that wells up from deep inside our spirits. He is overjoyed; therefore, we experience that joy (remember it is no longer I who live but Christ who lives in me – Galatians 2:20). The psalmist confirms this:

> "*You will show me the path of life; In Your presence is fullness of joy; At Your right hand are pleasures forevermore.*" – **Psalm 16:11 NKJV**

If we love God and remain in His presence daily, we will be a joyful people, not unsettled by any event that happens in our world. God wants us to experience that joy. It is part of who He is. It is faith building, character building and relationship building.

Joy is part of the overflow; a manifestation of our intimacy with Him. The more we know Him though our love relationship with Him, the more joyful we become. The more we know Him, the more faith and complete trust we have in Him.

Chapter 8: Tying It All Together

~~~~~~~~~~~~~~

In order to have faith, you need to be able to trust totally in God, so much so, that your confidence in God's character, His love for you, and His ability, is totally unshakable. Faith depends on how you view God and how you see yourself in His eyes. Therefore, knowing God is imperative. It all comes down to what you know of Him through the Word of God AND your relationship with Him. I might even go so far as to state that those with the greatest faith are those that know Him best. It all depends on you, and how deeply are you prepared to go with God. How much priority does He hold in your life?

Faith is also closely linked with Hope, which also lies firmly on a foundation of love and your relationship with Him. It does not disagree with hope but the two complement each other. We have hope that "xyz" will occur and know in our hearts it will. Then, as "xyz" is about to manifest we have faith that it will come to pass, not because we believe in belief, but because we trust in God and His Word.

Faith can be easily side tracked in the same way that your relationship and time with Him is sidetracked by misinterpretations, distractions, sin and disobedience and unforgiveness. Therefore, it is imperative that we guard our hearts with all diligence.

However, it can be built up and established (Colossians 2:7) as we walk with Him, being rooted and grounded in Him, through intimacy with Him, through worship, and choosing to rejoice rather than grumble. It is deepened through
~~~~~~~~~~~~~~

our study of the Bible and added to, as we listen to the testimonies of the wonders God has done in the lives of others.

Here then is a summary for you to take away from this book:

Faith

* Faith is primarily about trusting in God's character. We know Him and trust both Him and His word.

* If it's in the Bible, you can pray with assurance that you'll receive because He said it, and His Word is absolute truth.

* There's a chain of command. God is the Ultimate power. There is no one above Him. God says it, it's a done deal.

* If it's not promised in the Bible, you can pray to find out whether it's within His will. If He answers, yes, we can pray knowing that He will grant us our request, because we know He is true.

* If we know it's true, we can put legs on our faith

* If the answer is "No!" we must be like Jesus and humbly accept God's will above our own.

* Have child-like faith that worships God in the waiting, and says no to negativity about God. God delights in our faith.

* God simply responds to faith no matter who is involved:

+ Receivers (the person being prayed for)

+ Pray-ers (the one laying hands and praying)

+o Intercessors (Two or more are pray together in agreement)

+ Gift of faith moments.

He just loves the fact that we are prepared to surrender all and trust Him. It speaks of our love for Him, and He delights in it.

Hearing God's Voice Clearly

Jesus stated that God's sheep hear their Good Shepherd's voice. (John 10:1-5, 14-16, 27.) You are His sheep and no exception. All we need to do is follow the 4 Keys as discussed by Dr Mark Virkler. They are:

1. Quiet yourself down and be still in His presence.

2. Fix your eyes and attention completely upon Jesus.

3. Listen for, and recognise God's voice in your heart and tune in to what He is saying.

4. Write down what God tells/shows you.

Of course, we then need to test the voice to ensure it is God Speaking.

1. Test the origins of the voice; is it spiritual or not?

2. Does it conflict with the Bible or the principles it upholds?

3. Does it contradict the character of God?

4. Test the fruit

5. Share it with your spiritual advisers.

On top of the hearing ability of all God's sheep, there are gifts given to us;

a) Motivational gift – by the Father at conception

b) Gifts of the Holy Spirit – by the Holy Spirit after salvation

c) Fivefold ministry gift – appointed by Jesus for the church

The Father's grace/motivational gifts (See *Romans 12:4-8*) are:

Prophecy,

teachings,

exhortation,

administration,

giving,

serving,

mercy,

The Spiritual gifts (See *1 Corinthians 12:7-11*) are:

<u>1. Revelation-gifts:</u>

Word of wisdom

Word of knowledge

Discerning of spirits

<u>2. Power-gifts:</u>

Faith

Gifts of healings

Working of miracles

3. Speaking/vocal-gifts:

Speaking in tongues

Interpretation

Prophecy

And finally, the Jesus gives the fivefold ministry gifts to the church (See *Ephesians 4:11-12*). They are:

Apostles,

Prophets

Teachers

Pastors

Evangelists

We should all hear our Good Shepherd's voice, but there are three other **distinct functions** of the *prophetic gifts*. As mentioned above:

> * The ability to "know" or discern on a personal level in a prophetic manner comes via the ***motivational gifts.***
>
> * The Holy Spirit also has a ***gift of prophecy*** that enables a person to "hear/see" and proclaim prophetic utterances over people and the local church.
>
> * The ***Office of a Prophet*** (5-fold minister) is a ministry that Jesus, Himself assigns to the church, to not only bring direction and correction to the local

church, but to teach others with clarity and understandably, how to operate in this gift.

You Can't Skip the Process

Just because you have the motivational gift of prophecy / perception, it does not make you a fivefold prophet. There is a process.

It starts with your *motivational gift* of prophecy which simply enables you to sense (and hear to a degree) in the spirit realm. This gifted person will naturally earnestly desire the greater spiritual gifts – particularly the vocal and revelation gifts. That person who has then been given the *gift of prophecy* by the Holy Spirit, may start out by giving personal prophecies, or having dreams and visions relevant to their own lives and/or others they know, but later they may progress to receiving other "words" or prophecies for the church. These may also manifest as dreams and visions, and should always be submitted to the oversight/headship for scrutiny before they are shared with the church at large. Once a prophetic person has *proven* their "worth", and their prophecies have also proven to be accurate, they may no longer be required submit the message of the Holy Spirit to leadership for approval, but allowed to present the message themselves to the congregation at the appropriate time within the service.

Eventually, they may find they begin to have a strong desire to train up others. This may be a *fivefold gift* beginning to emerge, but not necessarily. It is Christ that gives the fivefold gifts to the church. As such, the gift must be recognised and then appointed by headship. The fivefold prophetic gift is weighty, accurate, insightful, and generally aimed at the church rather than individuals. These prophets encourage others in their prophetic gifts. They teach/train up others in the best ways to use the prophetic gift, to further encourage others and thus, build up the body of Christ. They also provide heavenly insights into the direction church leaders should take and also see efficient ways to help apostles realign the church to the culture of heaven.

Finally, fivefold prophets that are recognised by many churches are often released to the greater global body of Christ. These are able to give the body of Christ directions, and even prophetic warnings. They are not self-appointed but recognised by all believers, as having this authority operating quite visibly in their lives! Their prophecies are very weighty and carry an obvious anointing of the Holy Spirit. They also have the ability to declare a thing and see it happen.

Moreover, the most important gift that should undergird everything you do, must be your love for God and for His people. Without love YOU are nothing (see 1 Corinthians 13:2).

You are the tool in His hand, for His glory! We partner with Him.

Guidelines, Checks & Balances

* What you listen too will affect how you hear

* The prophecy will ***never contradict the Bible*** – God's Words

* When starting out and as a general rule later as well, avoid giving words about ***mates, dates, and babes***.

* Do not give ***negative prophecies***. Prophecy is for

the building up of the church

* ***Refrain from speaking any kind of negativity over people, even in normal conversation.***

* Always be humble and ***remain under scrutiny and authority***. (Proverbs 15:22; 11:14)

For personal prophecies you receive from others, use the guidelines to help assess whether their prophecy is from God:

* Who they are these "prophets"?

* Are they recognised even within their own church?

* Are they under authority, or doing their own thing?

* Does it confirm things God has already spoken to you?

If not, shelve it until you've prayed into it and God has confirm/denied it.

Remember, this is not a gift for your own personal use but to use in ***partnership with the Holy Spirit and for His Glory alone***! It is a tool for the kingdom and will pass away. What matters most is your personal motivation when using the gifts (1 Corinthians 13:2), and that your heart is right before God!

Being able to hear God accurately, will enable you to stand unshakably on the words and promises that God gives you personally, knowing that He is faithful, reliable and totally truthful. If you are constantly disappointed, you are either incorrectly basing your faith on a false premise, have misunderstood what God was trying to tell you, or have not heard God at all. Better to get it right first time around. :)

Hinderances

Unfortunately, besides not hearing correctly what God is speaking to you, there are other things that prevent you from stepping into faith, and only a hard, honest look at yourself can truly determine just what your hinderances might be and how you can deal with them. These can include:

> * **Fear & Worry** – these speak loudly of lack of trust in God. We are often powerless to change our situation, and instead of leaving it in the hands of God, we allow fear into our hearts and become anxious and worry. True knowledge of God and love for Him will build our trust and eradicate fear and worries.
>
> * **Disappointments** – Repeated disappointments are faith diminishing. They often occur because we don't wait to hear God's thoughts on a matter and want things our way. Promises in the Bible are dependable and yes, we can have them. However, the things that are not in the Bible need to be discussed with God. Is He happy for you to have certain things? Sometimes we have mis-heard God, or been given a false prophecy.
>
> * **Delays** – Delays can be because God's timing is not yet, or because we in ourselves are not ready or properly prepared. However, it can also be caused by the unseen spiritual enemy who does not want you to take receipt of your prayer.
>
> * **Lack of Persistence** – Jesus told us to be like the persistent woman. The enemy wants you to doubt God and give up your eternal inheritance by walking away from God. Thus, we need to be like Daniel and

keep praying until we know that we know, and then give thanks to God for His benevolence and generosity towards us.

* **Disobedience & wilful sin** – Sin and disobedience speak loudly of a problem with the heart and in the relationship with God. As stated, those with the greatest love and intimate knowledge of God, will not want to sin or disobey Him, and they will also have the greatest faith in Him. Conversely, when we wilfully sin, it speaks of a lack of trust in God and lack of personal knowledge about Him. We think our own way is more beneficial to us than God's and so we take matters into our own hands rather than to trust.

* **Entanglements** – Entanglements demand our attention and steal our love for God, because in essence, they cause us to commit spiritual adultery with them. The more we spend time in God's presence, the more we desire Him. Conversely, the less we give of our love and ourselves to God, the less we desire to give to Him. If we are giving over our time and energies to other things and not God, our desire for Him is drained, and our heart lamps will dim. Subsequently, when we have little, or greatly divided love (*the Bible says we cannot serve two masters – Matt 6:24; Luke 16:13*), faith, being based upon love, will also be affected and dimmish a long side it. We must therefore, make a choice to not follow when we are tempted, despite everything in our heart screaming to the contrary. Otherwise, our eternity may be at stake, let alone the fact that we will in no way be able to hear the voice of God, nor have faith to receive anything from God.

* **Unforgiveness** – this displeases God big time. Not being *willing* to forgive will ultimately hurt us, (physically, emotionally and spiritually), and cause great roots of bitterness to grow in our hearts. God has forgiven us unconditionally – even though we were filthy with sin and without hope, He still made a way for us. He expects us in turn, to do the same to others – i.e. forgive them unconditionally.

Unforgiveness is not something you have the luxury of holding on to until you're ready to give it, or until you feel better about things, or until you feel you've punished the other person enough. If that person comes to you seven times in one day, you must forgive them, no if's, but's, or maybes. You cannot protest, "*Give me a second*". No! They ask, we forgive. This is God's way. That's what He expects His children to do as well.

If we can't hear God's answers to prayers or see the results, we need to check if there remains any unforgiveness in our hearts. This is a major obstacle to faith, and will need to be removed before you can move forward in God.

Hope:

Our hope is not the hope of the world which is full of uncertainty. It is 100% certain.

Hope is grounded in God and **His character**. Those of the Old Testament witnessed the truth of God's promises as they repeatedly saw them fulfilled and thus, their hope was also based on the **evidence** they had seen.

We have that **same hope** in the New Testament. God **does**

not lie because He doesn't need to. It states clearly in the Word of God that this same hope is for us too. However, for us as New Testament believers, we have a **more certain hope** because of Jesus' saving work. His **resurrection** from the dead as the **first fruits** of all who die in Him, proving that **we too will rise like Him** into **our eternal inheritance in Heaven**. He has gone before us for He also entered behind the veil as our **Great High Priest** to make intercession for us. Finally, to seal the promises as certainties, He sealed us with the Holy Spirit as a **guarantee** of our inheritance with Him eternally.

Our hope is sure! It is the **anchor** for our soul that keeps us marching forward without wavering until we see that hope fulfilled. Hope has nothing to do with wishful thinking. It is certain and in this we take comfort.

Intimacy

Faith, hope and love are interlinked. Both faith and hope are determined by our love for God. Paul was correct in stating that the greatest of these three is love (1 Corinthians 13:13). Without love (and therefore, a personal knowledge of God) there can be no faith or Biblical hope. Paul goes so far as to say in 1 Corinthians 13 that without love we are nothing and those things we do amount to nothing. Love is the absolute requirement upon which our faith (and our lives for that matter) rests.

Often our faith is diminished because we do not understand how much God values us. We need to understand just who we are in God's eyes. This can only be found in His Word and in His presence. Reading those relevant Scriptures (See chapter 3: *The Intimacy Factor* under the heading, "*What Does the Bible Say About Me?*") and then meditating upon them, will build you up to have confidence before God.

Conversely, knowing about God is paramount. You simply cannot trust in an unknown. It doesn't work that way. Again, knowing all the Scriptures regarding God's character is extremely useful, but knowing Him personally is also important. This last knowledge can only be learned as you give Him your time in prayer, devotion and intimacy.

Worship is a wonderful avenue for expressing our love for Him. It tells God that He takes priority in our lives, more than our requests, more than our worries. It is an act of sacrifice and surrender to Him rather than giving ourselves over our own agenders. It is also an act of trust. Another benefit to be gained from worship, is that in reminding ourselves of the marvellous things God has done, is able to do, and will do, we build up our confidence and faith in Him.

Guarding One's Heart

When we guard our hearts from worldly influences and instead keep our eyes fixed on Jesus, it allows God to shape us - our character and personality, and even our heart's desires. When He talks to us, we will hear. When He directs us, we can follow. Guarding out hearts is vital for our maturity as Christians and will determine not only the state of our faith, but the very course of our lives. It will also ensure that when we really need to trust God and stand in faith, we will be able to stand firmly.

The biggest protection for our hearts, and thus, our faith, is our relationship with God. When we know through intimacy with Him, when we know His character, when we know His voice, and know His Word, we will also know who we are in Christ, and we will have armour clad ourselves against the lies and manipulation of the enemy of our souls. In the end, we can stand confidently before God without spot or shame, and in complete trust and faith in Him.

Faith Builders

Study the Word

Faith is built as we study and come to know well, the word of God. Those that know the word, know Jesus for He is the "Living Word". The Bible isn't just an inspired word. It is living and active, and sharper than any two-edged sword. (Hebrews 4:12)

Jesus as the Word of Life, and that the word was God (John 1:1). We must be blameless and hold fast to the Word of *life*, (Philippians 2:16).

This Word, Jesus, the Son of God, now lives in you. (Galatians 2:20) As we study look at Him through the Word, we are transformed into His image (2 Corinthians 3:18) this brings us understanding of who God is and why He does what He does. We also understand He is always right, and His words have always proven to be absolute truth! This is indeed faith building!

Without a relationship with God, it is possible to read the Bible and not see the truth it reveals. It becomes yet another book without the activation of the Holy Spirit.

Be Holy & Separated unto God

As Christians, we cannot ignore the call to be holy and separated unto God. This is not a choice, but because He has given us everything we need for life and Godliness, (2 Peter 1:3) and also His Holy Spirit for us to follow, it is *expected* of us. If we truly love God above all else, we will want to please Him – bottom line.

In order to remain holy, we must walk in the Holy Spirit. (Galatians 5:16) and thus, we will not satisfy the lusts of the flesh. This can mean saying no to our flesh, and demand a certain amount of self-sacrifice and self-discipline, but our love for Him makes this so much easier.

Jesus gave us this example in Gethsemane (Luke 22:42; Matthew 26:42). His love chose His Father's will first. Likewise, it is sometimes a sacrifice to choose Jesus and His will first. Paul also tells us that we are to be like living sacrifices – willing yielding up our will to do his and that as Christians this is reasonable (Romans 12:1).

Separation from sin, causes all other voices to fade or pale into the background, and gives us better spiritual clarity. This in turns allows our faith in Him to rise.

Worship & Intimacy

Drawing close to God in worship enables us to see Him as He is – His character, His great love for us, His reliability, His truthfulness and so on. It is a reminder that nothing is impossible for our God!! (Matthew 19:26; Mark 10:27; Luke 1:37) On these facts about God, we can securely and confidently base our faith.

Worship is for our benefit. It loudly tells the enemy what the truth of the situation is, and destroys his deceptions.

Encourage One Another

Reaching spiritual maturity requires mutual support and encouragement. (1 John 2:9-11) Being with others gives us shared views, insights and testimonies, and thus, deepens our understanding of God, and also enables us to overcome the enemy (Revelation 12:11). We celebrate God while celebrating each other's God given triumphs, and this in turn, builds each of us up in faith. (1Thessalonians 3:2)

Without consulting our brethren, lone-ranger Christians can easily fall prey to the enemy and his lies, but in the multitude of Godly Christian counsellors there is safety. (Proverbs 11:14). This is how we stay on the straight and narrow and dispel the lies the enemy whispers about ourselves and about God. It sheds light on the truth, and safeguards us against from losing faith.

When we love our brethren, it is a testimony to and an of the kind of faith we have. (James 2:18; 1 John 3:17,18) Our acts of love towards our brethren prove our faith in God. It is out of the overflow of our love for God that works are manifested. It is the fruit of love.

When we look like Jesus in our love for one another, we become a walking testimony that others see. This in turn encourages and builds up their faith as well.

Stir up the Joy

To delight ourselves in God suggests that we are confident and unworried about the outcome because God has this! It can be sometimes hard to let go and let God but the word "*delight*" in the verse from Psalm 37:4, suggests a we must make a conscious effort to rejoice.

The Scriptures often encourage us to rejoice in God. (see Philippians 3:1, 4:4). When we laugh, even in the face of adversity, it demonstrates a certain amount of assurance/confidence that God's got this! To laugh is to let go of the worries. It demonstrates we have faith in God, and we can therefore, relax, lean back into His strong arms, and enjoy the ride. (Romans 8:28) This pleases Him, because it is a demonstration of our faith. Joy is a characteristic of His true children, (Romans 14:17). Also, when we are joyful, we will also abound in hope (Romans 15:13).

It's not about faking it. His word was given that His joy may remain in us, and that our joy may be full (John 15:11). Therefore, since joy resides in our spirits, because Jesus and His word reside in us, all we need to do is to stir it up so that that which is already there, can be manifest in our flesh. (Psalm 16:11)

Practicing joy, produces unshakable faith. Moreover, joy is not only faith building, but character building and relationship building. It is an overflow from our heart and knowledge of God. The more we know Hom, the more joy we have, and the greater faith we will enjoy.

~~~~~~~~~~~~~~
~~~~~~~~~~~~~~

Other Books by Karen M Gray:

Save Your Marriage:

A Guide to Restoring & Rebuilding Christian Marriages on the Precipice of Divorce

This masterfully created and thoroughly researched book is a must for any marriage whether facing problems or just starting out. It is a resource that you could find yourself using again and again.

Answering tough questions whilst giving wise insight and understanding, this books not only deals with many of the problems facing Christian marriages today and how to overcome them, but provides ways to help marriages to heal and rebuild, even after suffering immense hurt and betrayal.

"*Save Your Marriage*" is available through Amazon, Apple ibooks and Barnes & Noble.

Spirit Led Worship:
How to Follow Where HE Leads

Worship leading under the direction of the Holy Spirit is less talked about than any other aspect of running a worship team. There are many conferences, and a plethora of books and videos available to Music Directors, regarding the best way to maximize the potential of the team, how to deal with personalities, about excellence and practice techniques, about you as a leader, coordinating the band, how to encourage your team, and so the list goes on. These are the workings or mechanics of running the team. When it actually comes down to learning to work with the Holy Spirit, there is a large silent pause.

In John 16:14, Jesus, speaking of the Holy Spirit, explains:

> "14 *He will glorify me, for He will take what is mine and declare it to you.*" – **John 16:14 ESV**

Given that it is the Holy Spirit who reveals God's glory to us, surely He should be in charge of our worship. Who better to help us worship as we ought? Who better to lead us into perfect praise?

This book is an attempt to correlate all the lessons the Holy Spirit has taught Karen over the years. It is through these lessons that Karen hopes that others will go on further than she ever did, bypassing the same mistakes, to run hand in hand with the Holy Spirit to even greater heights.

"*Spirit Led Worship*" is available through Amazon.

www.ingramcontent.com/pod-product-compliance
Lightning Source LLC
LaVergne TN
LVHW020707110826
845149LV00012B/2139

9780992354367